With characteristic rigor, clarity, and wit, Ross Douthat makes the case that being religious is, on balance, the most reasonable response to the intelligibility, mystery, joy, and sheer gratuity of existence. In these pages, he elevates our societal discourse about religion in a way that is disarming and helpful. If you are a thoughtful atheist, agnostic, or general skeptic, read this book. Its challenging insights will, at the very least, sharpen your thinking. And if you, like me, are a believer with doubts, surrounded by those who find traditional religious faith preposterous, read this book. It not only will engage your mind and strengthen your convictions but may even lead you into wonder and worship.

—**TISH HARRISON WARREN,** Anglican priest;
former *New York Times* newsletter writer;
author, *Liturgy of the Ordinary* and *Prayer in the Night*

If you are exhausted by the arid desert island of secular disenchantment, thirsting for transcendence but doubtful of your capacity to find God, reading Ross Douthat's *Believe* is like discovering a bridge to hope. Though he's a convinced Christian (who explains why in his luminous final chapter), Douthat's goal here to make basic theism more reasonable than atheism, and embracing a religious life engaged with a particular enduring tradition more sensible than spiritual novelty or moralistic therapeutic deism. Douthat's calm, analytical temperament, his intellectual humility, and his charity toward opponents make him a companionable guide for honest seekers. *Believe* is not only Ross Douthat's best book but also one that will make a life-changing difference for untold numbers of people trapped in epistemic bondage. For them, *Believe* is a golden key that will open a cell door that has been locked from the inside.

—**ROD DREHER,** author, *Living in Wonder*

Ross Douthat reveals how the growing ignorance of Christianity has created a void in modern life. With sharp clarity, he shows that the absence of faith isn't neutral, it's a loss that reshapes identity and the way the world is understood. This is an invitation to rediscover what has been overlooked.

—**LUKE BURGIS,** author, *Wanting: The Power of Mimetic Desire in Everyday Life*

At a time when strange things are happening, a time when even notorious atheists are willing to call themselves cultural Christians, there are some amazing opportunities for unexpected conversations between Christians and those outside the faith. That's where Ross Douthat's book is so useful. Like a modern-day Greek apologist, he makes a gentle and thoughtful case for religion in general and Christianity in particular. Christian readers will be helped both by his style and content to discuss their faith with the curious, and the curious will find much to make them think. And all of this comes with Douthat's customary clarity, wit, and precision.

— **CARL R. TRUEMAN,** Grove City College

Self-recommending. Some would say God recommends it too.

— **TYLER COWEN,** author, *The Great Stagnation*

In his famously readable style, Ross Douthat makes a persuasive case for traditional religious belief, one perfectly attuned to our cultural moment. Recognizing that the aggressive antireligious polemics of the New Atheists have worn thin, Douthat provides a road map for assessing "the God question" that will appeal to those who may lament the loss of a religious foundation for culture (and their own lives), but who cannot get over the line to personal belief. By highlighting new scientific discoveries that reveal a deep, underlying order and design in the universe *and* aspects of common experience that we often take for granted, Douthat shows that theism explains signposts to ultimate reality that the popular default worldview of secular materialism does not. Using an accessible commonsense style of reasoning, Douthat renders plausible and compelling what many today assume is implausible and untenable: traditional religious belief. A powerful, highly readable, commonsense guide to the most pressing questions of human existence.

— **STEPHEN C. MEYER,** author, *Return of the God Hypothesis: Three Scientific Discoveries That Reveal the Mind behind the Universe*

# Believe

# Believe

## WHY EVERYONE
## SHOULD BE RELIGIOUS

## ROSS DOUTHAT

ZONDERVAN
BOOKS

ZONDERVAN BOOKS

*Believe*
Copyright © 2025 by Ross Douthat

Published in Grand Rapids, Michigan, by Zondervan. Zondervan is a registered trademark of The Zondervan Corporation, L.L.C., a wholly owned subsidiary of HarperCollins Christian Publishing, Inc.

Requests for information should be addressed to customercare@harpercollins.com.

Zondervan titles may be purchased in bulk for educational, business, fundraising, or sales promotional use. For information, please email SpecialMarkets@Zondervan.com.

Library of Congress Cataloging-in-Publication Data

Names: Douthat, Ross Gregory, 1979– author.
Title: Believe : why everyone should be religious / Ross Douthat.
Description: Grand Rapids : Zondervan Books, [2025] | Includes bibliographical references
Identifiers: LCCN 2024041080 (print) | LCCN 2024041081 (ebook) | ISBN 9780310367581
    (hardcover) | ISBN 9780310367598 (ebook) | ISBN 9780310367604 (audio)
Subjects: LCSH: Faith. | Religion and science. | Belief and doubt. | BISAC: RELIGION /
    Christian Theology / Apologetics | RELIGION / Philosophy
Classification: LCC BV4637 .D66 2024 (print) | LCC BV4637 (ebook) | DDC
    231/.042—dc23/eng/2024100
LC record available at https://lccn.loc.gov/2024041080
LC ebook record available at https://lccn.loc.gov/2024041081

*Cover design: James W. Hall IV*
*Cover illustrations: Adobe Stock / Shutterstock*
*Interior design: Sara Colley*

*Printed in the United States of America*
24 25 26 27 28 LBC 5 4 3 2 1

*For my family*

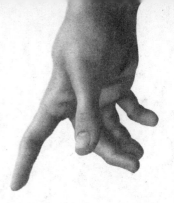

# Contents

# Acknowledgments

I'm grateful to Dan Greco for allowing me to inflict many of these ideas on a group of perspicacious Yale students, to my editors at the *New York Times* for allowing me to elaborate some of them in print, and to innumerable friends and some unsuspecting acquaintances for listening to me harp on these themes in recent years. (Special thanks to everyone who sighed and settled in when I got going about ayahuasca or near-death experiences.)

The book would not exist without Webster Younce's enthusiasm and editorial wisdom and Rafe Sagalyn's salesmanship. Special thanks to Patrick Hough and Yuval Levin and Francis Hittinger and Joseph Capizzi for friendship and institutional support, and to the Monks of Norcia for natural hospitality and supernatural assistance.

The rest of the thanks go to my family: to my parents for giving me wide horizons on the world, to my sister who knows how weird it gets, to Gwendolyn and Eleanor and Nicholas and Rosemary and Matthew for loving and tolerating their father, and to Abby for everything, always, eternally.

And God, of course: if the fear of the Lord is the beginning of wisdom, it's also a good spirit in which to end one's acknowledgments, especially for a book like this.

The world is charged with the grandeur of God.
    It will flame out, like shining from shook foil;
    It gathers to a greatness, like the ooze of oil
Crushed. Why do men then now not reck his rod?
Generations have trod, have trod, have trod;
    And all is seared with trade; bleared, smeared with toil;
    And wears man's smudge and shares man's smell: the soil
Is bare now, nor can foot feel, being shod.

And for all this, nature is never spent;
    There lives the dearest freshness deep down things;
And though the last lights off the black West went
    Oh, morning, at the brown brink eastwards, springs—
Because the Holy Ghost over the bent
    World broods with warm breast and with ah! bright wings.

*—Gerard Manley Hopkins, "God's Grandeur"*

# Introduction

For the last fifteen years I've been a conservative and religious columnist for the *New York Times*, a paper whose audience tends to be secular and liberal. Part of my job is to make religious belief intelligible to irreligious readers—both those who think of themselves as having grown out of faith's illusions or escaped its bigotries, and those who have barely any acquaintance with serious belief at all.

When I started at the job, the first group predominated among my correspondents: lapsed Catholics, secular Jews, erstwhile Baptists, people with some sort of religious upbringing who felt that they'd given faith a chance and reasonably rejected it.

Then over time, as churchgoing and church membership declined in the United States, I noticed more members of the second group: readers who seemed largely unfamiliar with basic tenets of Christianity, who had been raised with only a tenuous connection to institutional faith, whose knowledge of religion mostly came from history books and whatever they had picked up from friends and TV and social media.

The first group was more likely to be confident or even triumphant about their rejection of religion, and either baffled or bemused or simply irritated that someone could persist in believing in obviously mythological stories while claiming to have facts or reason on their side. I joined the *Times* around the heyday of the New Atheism, and for a while the combative spirit of figures like Christopher Hitchens and Richard Dawkins was evident in the emails I received, which were eager to inform me that organized religion is both stupid and wicked, that there's no difference between believing in God and belief in a Flying Spaghetti Monster, and that it was time to escape whatever miserable brainwashing I'd received and breathe the free air of atheism.

But even those emails were not always completely certain of themselves. Sometimes there was a friendly challenge: *Okay, smart guy, what's supposed to convince me that you're right about the Sky Fairy?* Sometimes there was a tinge of regret: *I'd happily go back to church, except for one small detail: we all know there is no God.* And over time, as the thrill of reading *The God Delusion* receded and organized religion entered into obvious cultural retreat, those themes of challenge and regret became more overt and commonplace.

More and more of my readers seemed to experience secularism as an uncomfortable intellectual default, not a freely chosen liberation. More and more seemed unhappy with their unbelief. And whenever I wrote about the decline of religion in America, and especially its decline among the educated classes, a rush of emails arrived from readers saying that honestly they wished they could believe, that they missed the consolations of churchgoing or envied people raised with some sort of belief—but still and all, isn't it just too difficult to be a thoughtful, serious modern person and embrace religious faith?

Over the same period a similar sentiment became notable in public debates as well. Looking at the forces—populism on the right, wokeness on the left—that had taken over Western life as traditional religion fell away, a number of writers, including even some New Atheist fellow travelers, acknowledged the naivete of the idea that simply removing Christianity or Islam from the stage would lead inevitably to greater enlightenment and peace. Relative to twenty years ago there is more discussion of the obvious sociological importance of institutional religion, its crucial shaping role in human culture, and its foundational place in the development of the modern democratic order. And there is more fear that a post-Christian or post-religious future might yield not liberal optimism and leaping scientific progress but tribalism, superstition, and despair.[1]

But there is also often a stopping short, a sense that any reconsideration of religion still runs up against the limits imposed by being a Serious Modern Person Who Doesn't Believe in Magical Nonsense. The serious modern person might believe that religious faith can be psychologically advantageous and necessary to human flourishing; he might set aside the animus of the anti-God brigade and embrace a more nuanced and potentially favorable view of religion's place in contemporary life. He might regard faith in the terms suggested recently by the *Atlantic*'s Derek Thompson, reconsidering his agnostic's assumption that the decline of religion was something to be welcomed: "Maybe religion, for all of its faults, works a bit like a retaining wall to hold back the destabilizing pressure of American hyper-individualism." Maybe we have "discarded an old and proven source of ritual at a time when we most need it."[2]

But that's still a long way from accepting that faith in its traditional form could accurately describe reality, that the God of the old-time sort of religion—supernaturalist and scriptural religion, angels-and-miracles religion, Jesus-was-resurrected religion—might actually exist, that religious belief might be not only socially or psychologically desirable but also an entirely reasonable perspective on the nature of reality and the destiny of humankind.

So the time seems ripe to argue exactly that.


At the peak of the New Atheist era, straightforward defenses of religious faith were at once oversupplied and underpowered, written from a defensive crouch that enabled some effective counterpunching but left the initiative to the enemies of God. (The subtitle of one of the better efforts, Francis Spufford's *Unapologetic: Why, Despite*

*Everything, Christianity Can Still Make Surprising Emotional Sense,*
gives you the flavor of those times.) Whereas the current moment,
rife with disillusioned agnosticism and reluctant nostalgia for belief,
seems suited for what this book offers. To atheists looking to be
unsettled in their certainties, to spiritual searchers struggling to
imagine a plausible destination, to believers wrestling with doubts
and difficulties, and to anyone interested in the ultimate questions
about human life, it makes the case that religious belief is not just an
option but an obligation—and offers a blueprint for thinking your
way from secularism into religion, from doubt into belief.

But maybe not the blueprint you'd expect. In contemporary
arguments with atheists and skeptics, religious writers tend to make
a few familiar moves. One is to insist that both critics and defenders
of religion spend too much time focusing on dogmas and doctrines
and specific claims about reality, when religion should be understood
primarily as a practice, a habit of being that can be fully understood
only communally and liturgically. In 2009's *The Case for God*, which
offered a warm cup of soup for the skeptical soul, Karen Armstrong
chided the New Atheists for trying to have an argument about beliefs
in the first place: "It is no use magisterially weighing up the teachings
of religion to judge their truth or falsehood before embarking on a
religious way of life. You will discover their truth—or lack of it—only
if you translate these doctrines into ritual or ethical action."[3]

To people who hover on the threshold of religion, open to belief
but unable to quite get there, the implied advice is to set aside your
skepticism, swallow your doubts, and just act as if you actually
believe: pray and go to church, love your neighbor, sing the hymns
or keep kosher, immerse yourself in religious literature and art, try
to reap the psychological and communal benefits of faith. The idea is
to embrace religious practice somewhat in defiance of the reasoning
faculties, making experience rather than argument your guide, and
see what happens next.

This book, too, will urge fellowship and ritual and practice as essential aspects of the religious quest. But it will insist that you can also do some weighing up and reasoning in advance, that joining and practicing is fundamentally a rational decision, not just an eyes-closed, trust-your-friends-and-intuitions jump. It will qualify Armstrong's description of traditional religion as not "something that people thought but something they did" by arguing that thinking about religious questions first is a pretty good idea, because thinking can make faith feel less impossible and more sensible, less absurd and more essential.[4]

The alternative, a fake-it-till-you-make-it argument which treats religious belief as desirable but nonrational—a leap into mystery, a rejection of evidence and empiricism—concedes far too much ground to skeptics, and cuts away the foundation of basic reasonability on which spiritual exploration and experiments should rest. Not surprisingly, for many people this approach just leads to disappointment and eventually back around to simple unbelief. Or alternatively, it encourages an attempt to extract some useful, therapeutic element from faith and leave the rest aside.

That is not what I'm urging here. This isn't a book about how religious stories are psychologically helpful whatever their truth content, or about how religious communities offer a valuable solidarity even if their doctrines are made up, or about how embracing the mystery of existence can make you happy in the day-to-day. Such benefits to religion clearly exist for many people, but those benefits accrue precisely because religious perspectives are closer to the truth about existence than purely secular worldviews. And the benefits are not the best place to start, if we're after something more than just contentment and good vibes. Rather, we'll start with religion's intellectual advantage: the ways in which nonbelief requires ignoring what our reasoning faculties tell us, while the religious perspective grapples more fully with the evidence before us.

But when I invoke reason here, I don't mean some incredibly complex or multilayered argument of the sort that only a great philosopher could understand. This has also been a common move by religion's defenders—conceding that faith may appear irrational in its more simplistic formulations but insisting that at a higher level of sophistication religious arguments become harder to refute. It's an intellectual's answer to an intellectual challenge, urging atheism's advocates to stop fighting with crude-minded fundamentalists, and reckon instead with Maimonides or Kierkegaard or whichever profound religious thinker you favor.

"What, one wonders, are Dawkins's views on the epistemological differences between Aquinas and Duns Scotus?" So began Terry Eagleton's caustic 2006 review of *The God Delusion* in the *London Review of Books*. "Has he read Eriugena on subjectivity, Rahner on grace or Moltmann on hope? Has he even heard of them? Or does he imagine like a bumptious young barrister that you can defeat the opposition while being complacently ignorant of its toughest case?"[5]

Obviously I agree with Eagleton that there are sophisticated and subtle philosophical arguments for religious belief. But this book offers a more straightforward and sometimes unsophisticated case. I have personally never read Eriugena on subjectivity, I defer to others on the proper interpretation of Duns Scotus, and we won't be reckoning with the ontological proof of God's existence or seeking a resolution to the debates over divine simplicity. Instead, we will begin with the basic reactions to the world that lead people and cultures toward religion, and argue that these are solid grounds for belief—indeed, more solid than was apparent at earlier stages of modern history and scientific progress. Reason still points godward, and you don't have to be a great philosopher or a brilliant textual interpreter to follow its directions. Ordinary intelligence and common sense together are enough.

One of this book's recurrent themes is that if the religious perspective is correct, its merits—and with them the obligation to take religion seriously—should be readily apparent to a normal person, to a non-genius and non-mystic experiencing human life and observing

the basic order of the world. The skeptic's question, "If some ultimate reality exists, why don't we know about it?" should have as its
answer that we *can* know about it, to some degree at least. Whatever
mysteries and riddles inhere in our existence, ordinary reason plus
a little curiosity should make us well aware of the likelihood that
this life isn't all there is, that mind and spirit aren't just an illusion
woven by our cells and atoms, that some kind of supernatural power
shaped and still influences our lives and universe. The world as we
experience it is not a cruel trick, our conscious experience is not a
burst of empty pyrotechnics in an otherwise-illimitable dark, there
are signs enough to point us up from materialism and pessimism and
reductionism—signs that most past civilizations have observed and
followed, signs that we have excellent reasons to follow as well.

How they should be followed, what happens after you accept
the obligation, is another matter, and this is the third place where
this book departs from many defenses of religion. I am a believing
Christian, but I am not attempting a wholesale defense of Christianity
here, or mounting a traditional apologetic case. I think our moment
could use something more basic, an argument that tries to lay a general foundation for religious interest and belief, to persuade skeptical
readers that it's worth becoming a seeker in the first place, and to
provide guideposts and suggestions for people whose journeys begin
in different places or take them in different directions.

Many arguments for Christianity (or for other faiths as well) take
as a given a religious or religion-friendly common culture that no
longer exists, particularly among the general book-buying public in
the Western world. So it seems reasonable to start at a more fundamental level—with mere religion, not just mere Christianity—and
work our way upward to the questions and choices where the great
faiths differ and part ways.

This of course raises the question of what defines "religion" or
a religious perspective on the world. Is Taylor Swift-ism a religion?
Scientology? Pastafarianism? But just as I'm defending the simpler

and commonsensical arguments for becoming a believer, I'm also defining religion in the basic way that most people would recognize and understand: a system of belief and practice that tries to connect human beings to a supernatural order, that offers moral guidance in this world and preparation for the possible hereafter, and that tries to explain both the order of the world and the destiny of humankind. Most of my examples will be drawn from the world's major faith traditions, the kind that show up on a "Coexist" bumper sticker, and indeed my argument will defend privileging those major traditions on any starting-from-scratch religious quest. And where the lines blur a bit, where it's hard to tell a philosophy from a cultural folkway from a religion qua religion, I'll be defending beliefs and practices that fall squarely on the supernatural and dogmatic side: real belief in a creator God or ghostly ancestors or a divine pantheon, real commitment to following Jesus or Muhammed or the Buddha, not just general ideas about the good life or cultural practices that you'd like to see handed on.

Of course since I *am* a Christian, there is no way for me to be perfectly fair to the other religions I'm discussing, especially at the level of generality that this book is aiming for. No doubt some of my analysis will seem wrongheaded or caricaturing to a serious Muslim or Hindu or Buddhist, and if you feel tempted to read my defense of belief as a work of Christian apologetics in disguise, a subtler path to a predictable destination—well, I can't help that, and maybe it's true.

But my aim is for this book to be useful to readers who might take many different religious paths. The first three chapters make the case for taking a religious perspective seriously, covering the evidence for design and purpose in the universe and the indicators that human life was specifically selected for by this design; the way that human consciousness serves as a strange key fitted to the order of the cosmos; and the persistence and credibility of spiritual and supernatural experience even in a supposedly disenchanted age. The next four chapters provide a guide for moving from a general religious disposition to a specific religious practice: a case for joining a larger faith tradition rather than traveling solo on your quest; a sketch of the different issues, choices, and decision points that might push you toward one tradition or another; a consideration of the biggest stumbling blocks modern people face in accepting a religion; and finally a brief word of encouragement for the sojourner who feels like any religious choice is arbitrary.

Only then, in the last chapter, does the book become more explicitly Christian, analyzing my own Christianity within my taking-religion-seriously framework, as a case study of how a specific theological commitment maps onto the general arguments for religious belief. That analysis aspires to be nuanced and self-critical, acknowledging some of the difficulties that Christian belief presents. But there is no escaping its partiality, no refuge from its gospel message—unless you choose to close the book just before that chapter and let the general argument stand on its own.

A final point: I write as a defender of religious belief against secularism and materialism, but I don't think that writerly persuasion is going to make much of a difference to materialism's fate. The spiritual and supernatural never really go away, and already the time of the new atheism is passing; already mystery and magic and enchantment seem to be rushing back into the world.

Some of the participants in this transformation still imagine themselves to be the vanguard of scientific progress: think of the AI researcher meditating in the morning and using psychedelics on the weekends while he tries to conjure up a digital golem, a ghost in the machine. Others are uncertain about whether they're playacting the supernatural or really going in for it; the groaning bookshelves selling works on witchcraft and Tarot and astrology at my local Barnes and Noble cater to both dabblers and true initiates. But everywhere mysticism is on the march, spiritual experimentation is coming back, my unhappily agnostic correspondents are on the hunt for *gnosis*—the divine experience, the hidden architecture, the secret truth.

Which makes it especially important now to defend not just the spiritual but the religious—meaning not just the experience of the numinous but the attempt to think rationally about it, not just the personal pursuit of the mystical but faith's structured and communal forms, not just ideas about how one might encounter something worthy of the name of God but ideas about what such a God might want from us. And not just the kind of optimistic individualism that informs so much contemporary New Age and therapeutic spirituality but a view of the supernatural that acknowledges real dangers—threats to the soul as well as to the body—and offers wisdom and protection that in today's spiritual landscape are in dangerously short supply.

The supposed absence of such threats is one of the comforts, in a strange way, of atheism and materialism. Without eternal possibilities, the stakes of every human life are lowered: the soul that doesn't exist cannot be endangered or possessed or lost. The cosmos of John Lennon's "Imagine" is unfeeling and indifferent, but people singing "imagine there's no heaven" clearly feel some lightening of burdens. Whereas the possibility of an eternal destiny, as C. S. Lewis once pointed out, places a great "weight of glory" on even the most ordinary human life, a sense of overwhelming possibility and real peril intertwined.

Accepting this weight, living with it, trying to let the awareness of eternity shape your timebound life and choices—all this was once understood as an essential part of human maturity. Yet for some time now the educated world has cultivated the opposite perspective, where intelligence and seriousness is measured in how meaningless you assume human life to be. Predictably this perspective has not yielded greater human happiness. Fortunately, you do not need to embrace wishful thinking in order to abandon it.

As its promises of liberation dissolve, as unhappiness and angst and regret take over, atheism defends itself by pretending to be hardheaded, extremely serious, the price you pay for intellectual adulthood. It is none of these things.

It is the religious perspective that asks you to bear the full weight of being human.

It is the religious perspective that grounds both intellectual rigor and moral idealism.

And most important, it is the religious perspective that has the better case by far for being true.

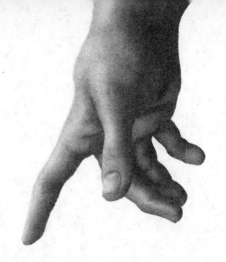

# 1

# The Fashioned
# Universe

In Tom Stoppard's 1972 play *Jumpers*, a philosopher ponders the apparent triumph of atheism over religious belief. "It is a tide which has turned only once in human history," he remarks. "There is presumably a calendar date—a *moment*—when the onus of proof passed from the atheist to the believer, when, quite suddenly, the noes had it."[1]

No one can agree on precisely when that date arrived, but a great many intelligent people believe in its existence. To them—perhaps to you—it's common sense that once there were sound-seeming reasons to take God and religion seriously. But now, in the light of science and evidence and rationality, we know better than our pious ancestors, and the persistence of faith is an example of wishful thinking keeping facts and logic and plain reality at bay.

So let's begin with this idea in mind. Whether you're a nonbeliever who takes this conception for granted or a religious person who feels that belief is meaningfully harder under modern conditions, I want you to imagine the world before that shift or turning point, when the burden of proof was on the skeptic, when atheism was a curiosity and supernatural belief the obvious default. This is a thought experiment, not an exercise in rigorous theological history, so you can close your eyes and enter whatever version of the past springs quickest to your mind. If you were raised with some form of religion, it could even be your own childhood.

Once you're there, try to imagine or remember what made belief seem so reasonable and natural. Try to imagine yourself as a religious person untroubled by serious doubts, finding natural vindication for spiritual presumptions in the world that you encounter every day.

Start with the physical world, the material universe that human beings inhabit and experience and study. What your naive religious self observes, at every level of visible existence, are regular-seeming, complex, and predictable systems: the progress of the seasons, the stars in their courses, the everyday workings of the human body. In your own embodied existence, you find yourself surrounded by complex machines of flesh and bone, filament and fiber—animals and insects, trees and flowers, their individual operations woven together in still-more-complicated ecosystems. And these systems don't just manifest a crude functionality; they often seem beautiful, graceful, and sublime, offering visions that even on an ordinary day can stir extraordinary awe, that both inspire and exceed the human capacity for art.

"The heavens declare the glory of God," the Bible says,[2] and when the biblical God wants to answer a suffering mortal's questions in the book of Job, He goes straight to this initial human intuition. The intuition that the world seems like a workshop and a cathedral and a theater and a machinist's shop and more. That nothing so vast and complex and beautiful could exist by simple accident. That either some Mind or Power must have made or organized all this matter for a reason, or else the Mind or Power is somehow inherent to the system, and the cosmos is itself divine.

From this perspective, you may still doubt the straightforward goodness of the system—because the world is so often painful, dangerous, tragic, a vale of tears—and question the perfect benevolence of whatever Power governs it. But that Power clearly matters to your existence in such a fundamental way that it would be strange not to wonder about its purposes or where you fit into them, self-defeating not to care about how your own life aligns with the story in which you have been placed. And when the story's Author speaks to you, as God speaks to Job and his friends, it's clearly a good idea to show a little respect.

So in this initial reaction, your naive self finds religion rational and necessary because you sense your own subordination within a higher order: you recognize yourself as a creature in a created landscape, a small participant in some grand design, a mind in some dependent relationship with higher minds or with the highest Mind of all.

But then imagine a second naive reaction to the world as it presents itself, which encourages religion for slightly more self-aggrandizing reasons. This is the sense that simply by virtue of being a human being, you seem to enjoy some kind of special connection with the powers responsible for everything, some link to the gods or the spirit of the universe or the Oversoul that not every created thing enjoys.

In feeling this swelling self-importance, your naive self still recognizes that human beings are part of nature, that we're one especially complicated part of the ordered system of the world. But the human mind also clearly stands at least a little way outside of ordinary nature. Even in childhood, you can feel your consciousness trying to step back and achieve a kind of supernatural perspective— analyzing, tinkering, appreciating, and passing moral judgment in the world. And from looking around at the animal and vegetative life with which you share the earth, this capacity appears unique to human beings—at least in its most dramatic, civilization-building form. Whatever you call it, self or mind or soul or spirit, something extra seems added to the human race, enabling us to understand more of the world than even the most intelligent of our fellow mammals— and also to invent and create within it, imitating the larger system's order and beauty on the smaller scales of technology and architecture, literature and art.

So if pondering the seeming orderliness of the cosmos, its complex detail and design, points to the existence of some divine intelligence, pondering the nature of the human mind points to the possibility that we are just a little bit divine as well. "Children of immortality" is how one of the Hindu Upanishads describes the human relationship to divine power; "in the image of God he created them" is the biblical phrase. These seem like boasts, but in our reimagined world where religion seems reasonable they are also just logical inferences, linking the palpable strangeness of human consciousness to the seemingly conscious ordering of the world. The creating Mind explains our creative mind, the Oversoul explains our soul—not only our wild experience of the world but our even wilder ability to (partially, gradually, incompletely) understand it.

Then, finally, positing a realm of supernatural mind above and around the realm of matter also explains a third feature of existence that makes your naive religious self feel justified in its beliefs: the fact the world seems not just ordered but enchanted, with many individually tailored signs of a higher order of reality. These come through the incredible variety of encounters described by words like *spiritual* and *mystical* and *numinous*, which vindicate religion through direct experience.

Your naive religious self may not have had these experiences yourself, but we are imagining a world that takes belief for granted, in which conversation and cultural wisdom make clear just how commonplace they are. Some examples of supernatural encounter might be especially dramatic—the psychic powers of the oracle, the miracles of holy men and saints, the brush with the ghostly or demonic. Others might be milder and more commonplace—mystical feelings of oneness and universal love, prophetic dreams and premonitions. The attribution and interpretation of these experiences might differ depending on the local theology and folklore; there could be talk of local gods and spirits, angels and demons, witchcraft and magic, the fairies or the djinn. But nobody would deny the availability of enchantment, the inevitability of transcendence sometimes breaking into the ordinary workings of the cosmos— the half-visible spiritual order over and above the hierarchies of the natural world. And even if you weren't especially interested in the supernatural, your religious self would understand that the supernatural might be interested in you—that experiences both remarkable and terrifying are not just available to anyone looking for them but also liable to come crashing through the everyday defenses of even those who aren't.

Such is one account, at least, of how a reasonable person on the distant side of Tom Stoppard's turning of the tide might have once accounted for their own religiosity, and considered a spiritual perspective to be the only sensible default.

Now open your eyes, leave the thought experiment, and let me try to convince you that everything you've just envisioned, all the reasoning you've just played around with, still fits the world you see today.

## What Really Changed with Copernicus and Darwin?

We'll begin with the first argument, the very old idea that the orderliness of the world bespeaks some kind of design, some supernatural intentionality or hidden mystical foundation. This belief binds very different religious cultures together across time, from classical Hindu sages to medieval Arabs and nineteenth-century Victorians, and it remains a default argument for religious apologists today.

But the default response is that this idea has been badly undermined by modern science. Two hinge points, the Copernican and Darwinian revolutions, are understood to have shifted the reasonable default to purposelessness and accident, materialism and atheism.

The Copernican revolution, in this narrative, replaced the cozy cosmos of medieval Christendom with something much wilder and sprawling, chaotic and terrifying and ultimately random. After peering through the telescopes that revealed the true scope of the universe, even believers were shaken by "the eternal silence of these infinite spaces," as Blaise Pascal put it. Meanwhile skeptics learned to roll their eyes at the idea that any special divine plan could attach to a species on a planet stuck in, to quote *The Hitchhiker's Guide to the Galaxy*, "the uncharted backwaters of the unfashionable end of the western spiral arm of the Galaxy." The fact that the Catholic Church tried and imprisoned Galileo Galilei, one of the men who opened this perspective on the cosmos, only confirmed the obvious: the astronomical breakthrough was a blow to the belief in divine design, and a definite strike against the human presumption that we enjoyed some sort of special relationship with the possible Designer.

Then what astronomy began, biology allegedly finished. The Darwinian revolution explained how complex organic life could evolve gradually, through mutation and adaptation, yielding designed-seeming intricacy at every level without any need for any form of guiding intelligence. This theory, Richard Dawkins famously crowed, made it possible at last to be "an intellectually fulfilled atheist," by removing the need for a conscious watchmaker behind the clockwork of the cell. And with the origins of human life reduced to material causality, the idea that mind existed independently of matter could likewise be set aside—just a mistaken intuition, an understandable misapprehension that turned out to be human egotism all along.

These are culturally powerful narratives because the revolutions they describe were real. Both Copernicus and Darwin profoundly unsettled specific world-pictures connected to specific religious cultures—the world-picture of medieval Catholicism in the first instance, that of early-Victorian Christianity in the second. Their revolutions shook existing syntheses of science, Scripture, and theology, undermined powerful-seeming paradigms, and proved authoritative-seeming theories to be questionable, insufficient, or simply wrong. It is not remotely surprising that each of them had a destabilizing influence on specific institutions, theologies, and religious loyalties.

But we are not concerned with cultural history or specific religious controversies in this phase of the argument. We are trying to start afresh, considering whether a general religious perspective makes sense before we consider Christianity or any other faith. The idea that the trial of Galileo might have unsettled the certainties of a sixteenth-century Catholic, or the Darwinian history of life the confident "natural theology" of a nineteenth-century Protestant believer, doesn't settle the first-order question about the wisdom of being religious any more than the unsettlement of a specific political consensus tells us anything about whether political ideas are worth pursuing. For a *general* religious attitude to be safely discarded as irrational, modern science would need to have proved more than just the fallibility of the Ptolemaic system, or done more than sow doubts about the historicity of the early books of Genesis. It would need to have demonstrated that it's a fundamental mistake to interpret the universe as a whole as something structured, ordered, seemingly artistically created and mathematically designed.

It has done no such thing. Indeed, to the contrary, the scientific revolution has repeatedly revealed deeper and wider evidence of cosmic order than what was available to either the senses or the reasoning faculties in the premodern world. This has been true from the very start, the Copernican and Galilean period, when one of the new astronomical perspective's earliest achievements was to reveal greater mathematical order in our own solar system, which had seemed relatively chaotic to the ancients, with planets charting seemingly irregular paths relative to the moon and sun and stars. Where once this irregularity had required a desperate piling on of complex epicycles to predict the motion of Mars and Venus and Mercury, the breakthroughs of the early modern era made it clear that planets followed a much simpler pattern of motion, the ellipse—which of course itself had been discovered by ancient mathematicians, unaware that they were anticipating a heavenly order that only the telescope would fully reveal.

The same pattern has repeated itself throughout the modern scientific era, as we have moved from a landscape where human beings could only see the order on the surface to a world where we understand order at much deeper levels—the level of cells and atoms, physical laws and mathematical equations. Sometimes this progress has set aside older speculations about the ordering of nature—the theory of the four humors, to choose a famous example. But it has typically replaced them with understandings that would have seemed more miraculously ordered to our religious ancestors: *Human health doesn't depend upon the balance of bile and phlegm, it depends on tiny warrior cells manufactured in the marrow of your bones going to war against infinitesimal invaders!* And the progress of science has been guided throughout by assumptions initially instilled by the religious perspective, which few of the original Copernican revolutionaries doubted—that the world at every level *should* be governed by predictable systems, that its ordering should be consistent across different regions and at different levels up and down, that it should reveal principles of remarkable symmetry and beauty to those who penetrate its secrets, no less than to the ordinary person staring at a butterfly, examining a diamond, gazing at a sunrise.

Was this perspective altered when the Darwinian revolution succeeded the Copernican? To some degree, yes. Prior to Darwin's account of life's slow ascent from bacteria to Bach, it was easier to believe in a kind of special creation, where having first made the cosmos God then sculpted each species in its finished form, making every plant and animal's mere existence a standing proof of the miraculous. The mechanism of evolution by natural selection, by contrast, made such specific miracles unnecessary for the emergence of complex life, and made the deep complexity of, say, all those tiny warrior cells look less obviously fashioned. And it also raised new questions about the moral structure of the cosmos by making ruthless, life-and-death competition the engine of life's evolution—thus challenging the Christian idea that strife and suffering and death itself entered creation only with the first human couple's sin.

So Christian unsettlement in the wake of such a revolution made sense, and you could reasonably argue that Darwin's theory made rival religious doctrines somewhat more compelling, including heterodox readings of the book of Genesis, non-Christian forms of monotheism (original sin is not a Jewish doctrine), and more pagan and pantheistic alternatives.

But what Darwin's big idea emphatically did not do, despite the confident claims so often made on its behalf, was explain away what ancient Hinduism called *rta*, the fundamental ordering principle of the world. It did not explain the law-bound material substructure required for evolution to take place, or the equations governing the cosmic superstructure, or the enduring evidence for mind as matter's ultimate foundation.

Darwinism established, with uncertainties around the edges of the theory, that an algorithmic process running over an extended period of time can generate increasingly complex and increasingly diverse machines made of cells and atoms. From small acorns, mighty trees; from the building blocks of life and the complex pressures of Earth's environment, stags and fungi, orcas and armadillos, praying mantises and human beings.

But those building blocks, that orderly environment, the system of the world in which the algorithmic process takes place, Hinduism's *rta*—all this Darwin assumes as a given, not explained as the result of a blind process in its own right.

In the famous analogy from pre-Darwinian natural theology, a watch discovered lying in a forest tells you that there must be a watchmaker somewhere—and similarly, observing the machinery of creation implies the existence of a divine creator. This argument changes, but it does not simply vanish in embarrassment in the light of natural selection. The Darwinist claim is that the forest is actually a long-running program that generates watches and many other complex things—a system of ongoing creation. But the law and order and complexity of that larger system still cry out for explanation; instead of a watchmaker, you need a factory builder or computer programmer to set the whole thing running. Or put another way, the complex watch that you need to explain isn't the individual body of an ape or armadillo; it's the larger life-generating system of the universe itself.

Which, it should be stressed, isn't a full break with the way many pre-Darwinian religious philosophers already thought about the world. The idea that God relies on secondary causes, not just a constant string of miracles, to bring about His intentions in the world, was a staple of religious arguments long before evolutionary theory came along. And while the complexity of bodily life certainly made an appearance in traditional arguments from design, ancient and medieval sources were more likely to cite the broad physical order of creation than the systems of biology—in part for the excellent reason that in those days a great deal of microscopic order was invisible.

This is not to say that these religious arguers were proto-Darwinists, or that they agreed with one another about the precise relationship between divine creation and the outworking of natural processes in the created world. Thomas Aquinas has a sophisticated theory of the relationship between primary and secondary causes, between God's action and natural processes, that has been adapted by religious believers interested in reconciling Catholicism and Darwinism.[3] But Aquinas personally argued that Adam and Eve were formed directly from "the slime of the earth." Or again, elements in Hindu thought seem to prefigure an evolutionary understanding of human origins, arguably more so than in Western monotheism—but the fact that you can read elements of modern science back into some Hindu scriptures doesn't mean that the Bhagavad Gita anticipates evolution by natural selection.

The key point, though, is that what really made the evolutionary idea novel, relative to older understandings, is not the idea of gradual development within an ordered system. It's that Darwinian theory let skeptics and materialists argue that an important part of the system works blindly, with no certain destination in its process. The program that generated human beings could have just as easily generated talking dogs or a planet filled with jellyfish. (Indeed, it did generate a planet full of dinosaurs, before a different blind trajectory intersected with our own.) And drawing implications from this blindness could get you to a limited form of reasonable skepticism: not the strong disbelief that many evolutionists embraced but a more modest doubt about the importance and significance of human beings within the cosmic order. This could then be combined with the wild scale of the cosmos discovered by the astronomical perspective to further minimize the human position, making our lives seem more contingent and our prayers and rituals and immortal longings correspondingly more useless.

Perhaps some godlike originating intelligence exists, this kind of skepticism might say, but Darwinism gives some strong reasons to assume that the evolution of life on earth is basically random, that human beings are accidents not endpoints, and our infinitesimal position within the vast expanse of space confirms that insight. So even if there's some sort of intentionality at the deepest level, some God of the physicists, whatever that Mind may have in mind probably isn't carbon-based life forms on the fourth planet from a minor sun.

Or as the physicist Steven Weinberg put it in his 1992 book *Dreams of a Final Theory*, "If there is a God who has special plans for humans, then He has taken very great pains to hide His concerns for us. To me it would seem impolite if not impious to bother such a God with our prayers."[4]

But even this more modest Darwinian reason to reject religion runs into its own difficulties, because much of what we've learned *since* Darwin about the deeper cosmic order that makes the evolutionary process possible suggests that Weinberg's God had special plans for us all along.

## A Cosmos Made for Us

The first blow to the idea of an indifferent cosmos was the twentieth-century realization that our universe appears to have a specific beginning, a point of origin prior to which not only space but time itself did not exist. If Darwin's theory arguably undermined a traditional Christian understanding of human origins, then the Big Bang theory offered a striking support for the Christian understanding of cosmic origins—offering particular vindication to Augustine of Hippo, who insisted in the fourth century AD that God created time as well as space *ex nihilo* and exists outside both, in contrast to pagan critics of Christianity who assumed that the universe had to be eternal.

That pagan presumption eventually became a presumption of modern materialist science as well. ("To deny the infinite duration of time would be to betray the very foundations of science," the physicist and Nobel laureate Walther Nernst insisted in 1938.) Like Darwinian theory, the idea of an eternal universe did not do away with the argument for divine design, since a timeless ordering would still cry out for some equally timeless cause. (Aquinas was open to an eternal universe in theory, and asserted that the only way to know that the universe had a temporal origin was through divine revelation.) But an infinite chronology added a third dimension to the case for human insignificance. Not only was our presence blindly generated, not only was our physical scale microscopic relative to stars and galaxies, but even our position in time was entirely random, as any position along an infinite timeline has to be.

On the other hand, to acknowledge a point of origin, to recognize a moment of creation, makes it intuitively more likely that the universe as we know it now has some specific importance to its creator—that any divinity isn't just perpetually emanating or sustaining space and time, but using them to tell something we would recognize as a story.

But it's the ordering of space and time, not just their origin, that has really renewed the case for humanity's importance. It's not just the expectation of lawful structure and mathematical beauty that has been vindicated over and over again as we have cast our gaze into the deeps of space and cracked the nutshell of the atom. Our expanding horizon of knowledge has also consistently revealed a system that's precisely balanced, exquisitely poised, in the alignments necessary to generate our specific kind of biological life.

This was by no means the expectation. Many twentieth-century physicists aspired to discover a fundamental theory that made all of the physical laws of the universe necessary and inevitable, rather than being any kind of accident—or worse, some sort of free creative choice. Yet instead it appears (provisionally, provisionally) that there could be many self-consistent universes, each with a somewhat different set of fundamental properties, bounded always by the Platonic forms of mathematics. And the properties that were, shall we say, "selected" to govern the universe that actually exists happen to be ones that fall within the narrow range—the very narrow range—that yields a universe hospitable to our kind of complex life.

In his 2003 book *Modern Physics and Ancient Faith*, still the most judicious and evenhanded treatment of these arguments, the religious physicist Stephen M. Barr offers eleven examples of these "anthropic" coincidences.[5] A few case studies: The cosmological constant, which governs the speed at which our universe expands, sits in a range that has roughly a 1 in 10 to the 120th power chance of occurring randomly. That range is essential to prevent both a flying apart and a swift collapse, both of which would have doomed the development of anything like life. Or again: were the nuclear force, the force that binds protons and neutrons inside atoms, just fractionally stronger—a "fraction" that can be represented by the equivalent of moving less than one inch on a ruler the size of the universe itself—it would have eliminated all of the hydrogen atoms in the very earliest phase of the universe; no hydrogen, no water; no water, no us. A similarly fractionally weaker nuclear force wouldn't hold together the particles in atomic nuclei in the way that yields chemical compounds necessary for life. The relationship between gravitational force and electro-magnetic force occupies an extremely narrow range that allows for the formation of the kinds of stars whose eventual explosions yield chemicals required to support biological life, as well as the kinds of stars that form planets like ours.

Barr notes that the exact number of fine-tuned conditions isn't stable or certain, since science aspires to parsimony and some of these coincidences could turn out to be mutually dependent. But however you draw up the list, it seems clear that our universe is held together by a set of seemingly excruciatingly carefully chosen values that, were they arranged infinitesimally differently, "would give rise to universes that, although they might be very beautiful, would contain no one able to wonder at that beauty," as Stephen Hawking wrote in *A Brief History of Time*.[6]

Far from being an inevitable byproduct of the mathematical structure of reality, then, from the point of view of life-creation ours looks like a peculiar sort of "jackpot" universe, in the phrase of the physicist Paul Davies.[7] True, the exact endpoints of the evolutionary process may or may not have been built in. Maybe God really is indifferent to whether the most complex forms of life look like elephants or crocodiles or hominids or highly intelligent jellyfish. Or maybe (as some evolutionary theorists have suggested) certain recurring developmental paths are built into the laws of chemistry and biology, such that evolution yields similar solutions under different circumstances. But the underlying process itself was set in motion, the automated watch factory started its work, only because of essential preconditions whose appearance was the equivalent of selecting the most improbable winning number in the largest Powerball drawing in the history of the world.

"A commonsense interpretation of the facts," astrophysicist Fred Hoyle once wrote of these peculiar fine-tunings, "suggests that a superintellect has monkeyed with physics, as well as chemistry and biology, and that there are no blind forces worth speaking about in nature."[8] And what this superintellect seems to have been careful to allow for, on the evidence of all the fine-tuning's special relationship to our own condition, are planets like Earth, living creatures like Earth's menagerie, and conscious beings like, well, us.

Add to this the further peculiarity that, so far as we can tell, there aren't a lot of other worlds where our kind of consciousness appeared—the kind that's capable of building civilizations that can send signals and messages and ships out into the forbidding deeps of space. We are not definitively alone in the universe; our tools of observation and exploration are too primitive to leap to that assumption. It's always possible alien civilizations are conducting some kind of careful communications blackout while studying us in secret, and certainly most people who believe that the UFO phenomenon—from strange crafts to weird encounters—corresponds to actual extraterrestrial civilizations have to assume exactly that.

But many aspects of UFO culture seem to belong more to the realm of religious and spiritual experience (to be considered in a later chapter), and the basic takeaway from the scientific search for extraterrestrial life is still the one distilled by Enrico Fermi almost eighty years ago: If conscious life is commonplace, if earthlings aren't especially distinctive or unique, then "where is everybody?"[9] Not sending us messages, that's for sure, and their conspicuous absence suggests that the human experience is extremely distinctive, perhaps as statistically distinctive in its own way as the fine-tuning that allows our existence in the first place. It suggests that we are one of the first and only races in all the cosmos to ascend to this level of competence and understanding. Because otherwise even the parts of the cosmos we can access would be crowded with various communications, if not actual spacefaring races, after so many billions of years.

In this sense, the one aspect of the religious perspective that arguably was taken away by the telescopes of the sixteenth and seventeenth century—the privileged position of our terra firma in a cosmos forged with humankind in mind—has been given back in a wilder way by a deeper scientific understanding of our situation. Earth is not the center of some tidy Ptolemaic system. But in a cosmos fine-tuned for life's emergence, it's the only place that we know of where that life has developed to self-consciousness – which makes it look once more incredibly distinctive, and the specific experience of homo sapiens even more so.

It would be presumptuous to say that we are the only point or purpose of this universe; too much remains beyond our sight and knowledge. But what we can see and know suggests that our conscious existence has some cosmic importance, some great consequence—that our minds are part of the reason, or deeply connected to the reasons, why all of this exists.

To this realization, modern physics has added one final twist: at the deepest level of existence that we can fathom, the quantum level of reality, the human mind seems to play some decisive role in making physical reality take actual shape.

Quantum theory is, from one perspective, the place where the scientific project's expectations of perfect order and law-bound pre-dictability have finally been disappointed, its questions answered by paradox and riddles. How can light be both a wave and particle? How can particles remain somehow "entangled" even when separated by a great distance? And above all—how can human observation be the only thing that transforms quantum contingency into definite reality, wave into particle, probability into certainty?

Scientists have labored for generations to explain these weird prop-erties in purely mechanistic terms. This includes the fascinating effort, which we'll encounter momentarily, to assume an infinity of universes to explain the seeming instability at the bottom of this one. But the simplest explanation is still the so-called Copenhagen Theory, named for the city where Niels Bohr and Werner Heisenberg did their pio-neering work, in which the conscious observer places a mysterious but essential role in collapsing quantum possibility into physical reality.

That simplicity, wild as it seems, returns us to the fundamentals of the religious perspective on the world. It's scientific evidence that mind somehow precedes matter, that our minds have some integral relationship to physical reality, and that what holds all of the physical universe in actual existence, not just mere possibility and probability, is some larger form of consciousness itself.

Spencer Klavan, in a recent essay on the long wrangle over quan-tum mechanics, makes the point this way:

It has become customary to speak of the universe as existing for "billions of years" before the advent of conscious life—an empty cathedral built by no one, hurled into existence by a great burst of energy. The various competing explanations of this process all depend on resolving the many quantum possibilities of a tiny infant universe into a timeline of definite unfolding events, from the appearance of the first photons to the blazing fusion that would eventually create the first stars. But since those possibilities are manifold and indeterminate until observed—since things like "years," "energy," "photons," and "atoms" are exactly the kinds of things that cannot quite exist unseen—it may turn out that we have been talking mostly about how these things *would* have behaved if there was someone there to watch them.

And "the most fearsome heresy of all," he concludes, "in an age committed to materialism, is that indeed there was someone there."[10]

## Why Don't More Scientists Believe?

A heresy it remains, which yields one intuitive response to this entire line of argument. Even supposing that many scientists would agree with how I'm characterizing their findings, clearly many would strongly disagree with the religion-friendly implications that I'm drawing. And I'm merely a layman interpreting (and dumbing down, and probably misunderstanding here and there) what science has worked out, while they are the people who actually do the discovering. So why are they much more likely than the general population to be atheists? If the universe is really so marvelously and obviously made, why aren't scientists the first to fall on their knees to worship its maker? If mind, both the human mind and whatever minds or Mind did all the ordering, seems integral to matter's purposes, why don't the people who study those purposes seem to think so?

In fact the famous atheism of scientists is not universal. It wasn't just the original Copernican revolutionaries who took their inherited religious perspective for granted; for hundreds of years thereafter the great project of modern European science was carried out by Christians (and, yes, Christian heretics) convinced that they were investigating the Abrahamic deity's grand design. And the further you get from the Western world's very specific history—our church-state controversies, our battles over evolution and education, our current culture wars—the more the tension between science and religion diminishes. In a recent global survey the largest religious-belief gap between scientists and the general public was in the United States; it was substantially narrower in places like Turkey and India and reversed in Taiwan and Hong Kong, where scientists are actually slightly more likely to be religious than the general public.[11] My strong suspicion is that the prevalence of stern atheists among American scientists is culturally contingent, and that a more natural intellectual resting place for a lot of working scientists would be some kind of deism or pantheism—an openness to a divine ordering joined to a doubtfulness about miracles and special revelation.

Still it's fair for skeptics to point out that many serious scientists would accept some of my account of what their discipline has revealed about the universe while firmly denying that it should inspire religious attitudes or vindicate religious assumptions. And for good professional reasons. Although the modern scientific project began with Christian assumptions about God as creator and designer, the everyday task of understanding how the universe works benefits immensely from excluding the idea of supernatural intervention. If you posit an angel stepping in to carry a planet through a particularly puzzling orbit, or postulate a miraculous intervention to explain some apparent gap in the fossil record, you are effectively stopping your investigation short. Time and again, pushing further has revealed some new discovery, some new material explanation, some new layer of order. Darwinian evolution stands as a special monument to this assumption, a case where miraculous creation seemed like a powerful hypothesis, but a scientific refusal to be satisfied with "and then God did it" reaped revolutionary results.

So over generations, this pattern has yielded an understandable habit of mind among scientists that rules out religion *a priori*, as a kind of violation of guild rules. "We cannot allow a Divine Foot in the door," the eminent biologist Richard Lewontin said, because science is in the business of figuring "the regularities of nature,"[12] and the introduction of any sort of divine rulemaker raises the possibility that at any moment they could be disrupted, suspended, broken—supposedly taking the entire scientific project with them.

Arguments about whether miracles and modern science are compatible will be considered in a later chapter. But a basic scientific default against considering divine intervention is reasonable so far as it goes, and it's psychologically understandable that such a default would create a bias against even general religious assumptions, those deist and pantheist alternatives I mentioned, lest they bleed down into the particular work that scientists are carrying out.

But that doesn't mean that it actually makes sense to base your own personal relationship to ultimate reality on what are, in the end, guild rules. It's been useful for the advance of knowledge for scientists to leave metaphysical possibilities out of their investigations. But it's obtuse to refuse to ever step back and interpret the results of those investigations, provisional as they may be, or deny their implications for understanding not just nature but nature's God. If the mantra "trust the science" means anything, surely it's that we should trust the discoveries made with the scientific method, the things that scientists have figured out, and base our provisional understanding of our situation and the world on those actual findings, rather than letting the framework of scientific inquiry—the lines within which the guild does its work—constrain us from ever stepping back and discussing what the inquiry reveals.

The attempt to sustain the guild rules against religion-friendly

Believe

interpretations yields obvious problems for scientists themselves. First, it generates philosophical confusion. As science has revealed the laws and equations governing the universe, some scientists have convinced themselves that laws and equations are somehow an alternative to an argument for divine intelligence rather than evidence in its favor—that if one could just reduce the entire universe to an original condition and a set of especially beautiful equations, one would have no need for a "God hypothesis" or anything so embarrassing.

The atheist physicist Lawrence Krauss, for instance, dedicated an entire recent book, *A Universe from Nothing*, to the proposition that the laws of quantum mechanics acting upon quantum fields explain the generation of the universe, and that this explanation suffices to settle forever the question of why there is something rather than nothing, why this something in particular, why material reality and all its wonders happen to exist.

But this was obvious rubbish, as his more acerbic critics pointed out, since nothing in his self-confident account explained why one could simply assume the laws and operations to which he was attributing the universe's emergence, let alone describe them as a "nothing" from which the entirety of existence somehow sprang.[13]

Other scientists are less presumptuous than Krauss, but even a figure like Stephen Hawking, whom I quoted earlier acknowledging the seeming fine-tuning of the cosmos and whose *Brief History of Time* expressed a reasonable agnosticism about what power, exactly, "breathes fire into the equations and makes a universe for them to describe,"[14] ended his career by arguing that the equations alone suffice, that the laws of physics can stand as an impersonal alternative to any kind of divine mind.[15] It's a very strange sort of claim: the equivalent of watching someone investigating the origins of a house, and upon discovering finely wrought schematics, exclaiming that now they have no need to assume the existence of an architect—when in fact they're looking at her work!

The second problem is that as science has pushed closer to the foundations of the universe, its need to exclude religious-seeming hypotheses has forced it to compromise its own originating principles—the preference for simple explanations over complicated ones, or the focus on the material and measurable over the purely speculative.

Such difficulties pervade the strongest intellectual response to all the apparent evidence for order and design and mind's decisive role: the various theories of the multiverse. These differ in the details but share the conceit that our cosmos is one of an infinite or near-infinite number of universes, branching out or bubbling away from one another. Our own human-friendly cosmos appears so orderly, so specially built for planets and life forms and seemingly designed for our emergence, for entirely accidental reasons, which we confuse with some kind of divine plan because we can't see the trillions of other cases with entirely different laws, different balances of forces, and no chance of conscious life. Meanwhile there may also be essentially infinite variations on our own universe as well, all existing simultaneously—and that coexistence, not any decisive role for mind in the material cosmos, explains some of the weird features of quantum mechanics, where the apparent instability of unobserved phenomena just reflects all the different possible universes that spread away from our every decision point and choice. Schrödinger's cat is dead *and* alive; it just depends upon which fork of the multiverse you take.

The multiverse concept has been a gift to superhero franchises (or a poisoned chalice, depending on your view of recent Marvel movies), but it's a very odd sort of scientific move. To escape the possibility of a single invisible God, it posits an infinite number of invisible universes that we can never hope to reach or see. To avoid the mind-preceding-matter immaterialism suggested by the universe's apparent fine-tuning and the strange role of human observation in collapsing potentiality into reality, it posits an infinite system that by definition cannot ever be studied from within our material existence. Far from imitating the original discoveries of Copernicus and Galileo, whose clarifying specificity swept away a whole edifice of hypotheticals, the multiverse conceit bears a closer resemblance to the various attempts to save the older Ptolemaic system—by adding cycles within cycles, wheels within wheels, or in this case universes upon universes.

Just as Darwinian theory did not actually resolve the metaphysical questions raised by the universe's beautifully ordered existence, these moves do not sweep away the persistent fingerprints of God. A religious perspective does not necessarily exclude the possibility that more than one universe exists. "There are innumerable universes besides this one," runs one Hindu text, "and although they are unlimitedly large, they move about like atoms in You."[16] The multiverse as usually described is still an ordered system in its own right, bound no less than our own universe by the laws of quantum mechanics and subject to the forms of mathematics. This raises the same predictable question about where these universe-generating laws and Platonic realities originate. Just as you can't have the "blind" work of natural selection posited by Darwin unless you have an orderly system in which to let the long evolutionary process work, in the multiverse hypothesis you can't produce the clockwork of our universe unless you have a clockwork machine that generates universes. So you haven't stripped things down to a self-explanatory simplicity; you've created a new insanely complex order that looks, no less than our own homely cosmos, like a system of creation.

But not one, might come the rejoinder, in which human beings matter much at all. By explaining away the human-friendly aspects of our own specific cosmos—the fine-tuning that yields water and Earth-like planets and evolutionary processes—the multiverse theory at least restores our cosmic insignificance, pushing any God once again further up and further away and making any divine purpose once again inscrutable and any religious attitude once again a waste of time and breath.

Except that if human intellects have actually pushed through the veils between the infinite universes and correctly hypothesized about something that we cannot hope to measure or observe, it would be an especially wild vindication of the second enduring reason to take religion seriously, to which we will turn next: the supernatural character of the human mind.

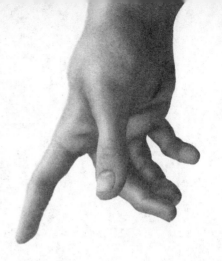

# 2

# The Mind and
the Cosmos

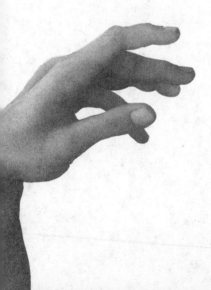

In 1996 Tom Wolfe saw the future in a brain scan. Writing for *Forbes*, in an essay with the puckish title "Sorry, but Your Soul Just Died," he predicted the ascent of neuroscience and the eclipse of every other theory of what makes human beings what we are. Subjecting the brain to scientific scrutiny, watching thought take physical shape inside the cerebellum, accepting the hardwired and chemical origins of our behavior, our memories, and our very sense of self—all this, his essay suggested, would be the final scientific revolution, the permanent triumph of cold materialism over every rival understanding of the world.[1]

The young neuroscientists Wolfe talked to were certain that it was all over for the misty metaphysical theories of the self. They were going to bury René Descartes' mind-body dualism in the same grave as Sigmund Freud's unconscious and the Christian soul. They could finally see inside the mind, they told him, and there was no ghost in the machine, no self apart from neurons. Why, Wolfe wrote, "neuroscientists involved in three-dimensional electroencephalography will tell you that there is not even any one place in the brain where consciousness or self-consciousness (Cogito ergo sum) is located." Checkmate, Descartes; checkmate, free will; checkmate, obviously, to souls and spirits and life-after-death speculations. Neuroscience would be the court of no appeal, the final proof that mind is always and everywhere reducible to matter.

"Eventually," Wolfe wrote, channeling this neuroscientific confidence, "as brain imaging is refined," our understanding of consciousness will "become as clear and complete as those see-through exhibitions, at auto shows, of the inner workings of the internal combustion engine. At that point it may become obvious to everyone that all we are looking at is a piece of machinery, an analog chemical computer, that processes information from the environment. 'All,' since you can look and look and you will not find any ghostly self inside, or any mind, or any soul."

The confidence Wolfe described back then is still alive. Every day brings some new claim about how neurochemistry affects mood and personality, how different MRI results correlate with different appetites or impulses or styles of thinking. Or how dramatic transformations of the self, like puberty or the passage into motherhood, are smoothed by hormonal shifts; how changes in our instincts and impulses correlate with growth or pruning in the brain; how when our minds change, the material substrate changes too. Or how a specific sight or a specific phrase can be associated with activity in a certain portion of the brain, enabling a crude sort of mind-reading via brain scan. Or how a certain thought might be associated with the firing of a single neuron, as in one amusing experiment published in *Nature* in 2006 where images of Bill Clinton and only images of Bill Clinton increased the electrical activity in a specific location in a human patient's brain.[2]

Meanwhile, the turn to neurological and biochemical theories of the self has been accompanied, as Wolfe predicted, by ever-increasing chemical treatments for the self's ailments—drugs for depression, drugs for hyperactivity, drugs for anxiety, drugs to sleep and drugs to focus. Theories of the id and the superego, the subconscious and the unconscious, to say nothing of ideas about divine grace and mortal sin, have given way to an image of the human being as a complex set of purely physical arrangements, in which unhappiness and ennui and desolation are chemical imbalances with mostly chemical solutions. Self-help writing, likewise, increasingly encourages the reader to think of the mind as either a chemistry set or a computer, where mastering the turmoil of existence is a matter of keeping dopamine levels balanced and doing some rewiring or software updates in the brain.

Then, most recently of all, breakthroughs in artificial intelligence research have produced vast neural networks made of silicon that can achieve imperfect but remarkable imitations of human conversation and creativity. When prompted appropriately, they can write college essays, compose poetry, answer historical questions, venture philosophical opinions, even make declarations of love. All at a level of sophistication that seems comparable to many human efforts; all with no act of ensoulment, no supernatural intervention, no bestowal of spirit from on high.

We may not yet quite grasp the workings of the mind the way we grasp the workings of an automobile engine. But with the new chatbots, surely we've at least built our first Model Ts, and proved that we're on the path to the soul's dismissal, the end of the idea that mind might be distinct in any way from matter.

## The AI Conjuring Trick

If you listen closely, however, you may notice something a little odd about the way that many of artificial intelligence's boosters talk about the new creation.

For instance, during the roll-out of the first superpowered AI chatbots in the winter of 2023, Henry Kissinger, Eric Schmidt of Google, and Daniel Huttenlocher of MIT wrote a joint essay in the *Wall Street Journal* marveling at the capacities of the new artificial intelligence.[3] At the heart of their wonder was the technology's air of mystery, its oracular quality, the way it seemed to break with the patterns of Enlightenment science, in which sequences of replicable experimental processes are supposed to yield results that are trustworthy and verifiable because we can see, step by step, how the entire process works.

With AI, by contrast, the systems can be so complex that we don't always understand how they are generating answers to our questions. (For instance, a diagnostic AI might outperform a human doctor in identifying a patient's medical condition without its engineers knowing what factors were actually crucial to the diagnosis.) There's a black box at the heart of the machine, a hard-to-pin-down element inside the algorithms.

For some AI researchers, this is a challenge to be addressed with further algorithms—AI to help us understand AI. But if you expect artificial intelligence to eventually generate artificial consciousness, then the black box might actually be a crucial breakthrough rather than a problem to be solved.

As the *Journal* essay-writers put it, our AI interactions will force us to ask constantly, "What about the machine has not yet been revealed to us? What obscure knowledge is it hiding?" This is an achievement, a win for would-be engineers of consciousness, because it implies we've built something mysterious, something with a touch of magic and conjuring about it, something that's as hard to fathom as—well, as, human consciousness itself.

We just saw how the multiverse hypothesis represents one endpoint for the modern scientific quest, where experimental methods hit their limits and we are forced to choose between different metaphysical visions to explain the fashioned-seeming physical order of the cosmos. But the quest to build an artificial intelligence also represents a place where the supernatural has returned to haunt the scientific project. In the case of the multiverse, the return happened because we now understand so much about the physical system of the world, and so what remains are the inevitable questions, "Why?" and "By whose hand?" In the second case, the AI project, we're returning to metaphysics and mystery because of how little we understand about consciousness, notwithstanding all the neuroscientific advances just described.

Far from representing the final triumph of materialism, the widespread expectation that AI is on its way to some version of self-consciousness (when an AI CEO polled his social-media followers in June 2023, 68 percent of the 2,300 respondents said they believed "that AI systems are either already conscious or soon will be"[4]) is actually a faith in a complex kind of incantation—a mystical summoning carried out in the name of science, but well outside its usual parameters.

Here the Model T analogy is entirely wrong. The architects of artificial intelligence still have no idea how to build a conscious self the way you might build an automobile engine—piece by piece and part by part, until the system is ready to be given a jolt of energy and spring into its work. Instead we are building machines that simulate the output of a human mind—writing, coding, poetry, encyclopedic answers, ideas for inventions and medicines, paintings, human conversation, dirty talk, jealous fits—through internal mechanisms that in their design lack any perceptual "I," any self that can step back from the flow and recognize its own mistakes, or hold a thought unspoken in its mind.

For some believers in artificial consciousness, the hope seems to be that if we make the output-generation process more and more complicated, so that the path from inputs to responses increasingly escapes our understanding, at some point there will be a shift that we can't see or measure, a mysterious synthesis that we can't understand, and an actual "I" will emerge inside the system, the way our own consciousness exists in some mysterious relation to our own machine of flesh and blood.

"Any sufficiently advanced technology is indistinguishable from magic," runs a famous line from the science fiction writer Arthur C. Clarke. His point was that advanced technology seems magical to the uninitiated, even if its adepts understand that it works through strict material principles. But the AI project is Clarke's idea made literal. It doesn't just resemble magic, it's hoping actually to do magic—by building a system that exceeds our understanding and then assuming that self-awareness will develop naturally from some consciousness-generating aspect of complex systems that we don't ourselves yet grasp.

In this sense the entire project half-accepts the second key premise from our initial thought experiment, the second idea that once made religion seem so rational and necessary—that mind is not reducible to matter in any way that we can ever expect to understand, that our selves are in the material world but not exactly of it, and that if you're looking for evidence of supernatural reality, your own mind's eye is a good place to start.

## The Mind Is a Hard Problem

All of this was clear enough around the time of Wolfe's essay; you just had to turn from *Harper's Magazine* to a paper published about a year later by the philosopher David Chalmers. It was titled "Facing Up to the Problem of Consciousness," though a more Wolfean title, "Sorry, the Soul Doesn't Die So Easily," might have suited just as well.[5]

In the paper, Chalmers drew a now-famous distinction between the "easy problems" involved in analyzing the inputs and outputs of the brain and the "hard problem" of how those inputs and outputs somehow give rise to conscious selfhood. The "easy problems" (which, to be clear, are easy only by comparison) are the kind that Wolfe's neuroscientists were bent on solving. Which neurotransmitters are associated with joy or depression, romantic love or maternal tenderness? Which experiences are associated with activity in which brain areas—with the amygdala, with the hippocampus, with Wernicke's area or Broca's area? Can we change conscious experience by changing brain chemistry, or by stimulating or shutting down portions of the brain? Can we correlate brain activity to specific words and images? Does everyone have a Bill Clinton neuron? (It turns out they do not.)

The hard problem is taking these correlations and using them to figure out how inputs and stimuli working on the underlying physical systems actually generate the experience of mind. It's one thing to say that electrical impulses in this or that portion of the cortex are associated with certain kinds of thought. It's quite another to explain how those impulses create all the subjectivities of human experience—the *cogito* of Descartes, the experience of agency and reasoning and judgment, the irreducible this-ness of sensory experience, which philosophers try to capture with the awkward term *qualia*, but that normal people know as the taste of wine, the scent of roses, the orangeness of the color orange.

You are experiencing the hard problem right now, reading these sentences and experiencing mental states as you move through them. Maybe it's confusion at my failure to adequately explain my point. Maybe it's a sense of recognition, an aha moment because I've crystallized something for you. Maybe it's furious disagreement, irritation at my manifest stupidity. But whatever it is, it's the kind of experience any reader knows well, a natural-seeming correspondence between ideas encoded on the page and a mind trying to follow them, that arises from—well, that's the issue. What *does* it arise from?

The fact is that we simply do not know. For all the advances in brain mapping, the mind itself is still irreducible, an enigma, a mysterious substance unto itself. Science can tell you how certain atoms in combination create water or carbon dioxide, or how mass and speed and distance combine to predict movements and trajectories, but it's powerless to tell you how the physical elements of book and brain give rise to the personal experience of reading. The ink on the paper, arranged in certain geometries, conveyed by light to the retina of your reading eye, transformed into electrical signals, carried along the optic nerve to the brain, yielding a specific burst of activity in some particular set of neurons—how does any of that produce the feelings we call confusion, recognition, disagreement? If reading an argument makes you angry, if reading a novel makes you sad, if reading a poem stirs a sudden childhood memory, there is no material account of how that happens, how the outward act generates the inner experience.

Note that I did not say *where* it happens. Again, the success of science in mapping brain activity means that we can say things, within limits, about the correspondence between certain mental states and certain regions in your gray matter. But as the neuroscientist and philosopher Erik Hoel points out, locating some aspect of a thing is not at all the same thing as explaining how it's generated.

"Here's a cruel parlor trick," Hoel writes. "Ask a neuroscientist to explain something about human cognition. Listen to their answer. Then ask them to explain again, but to say nothing in their explanation about location. The second ask is far harder, almost embarrassingly so (and I say this as a neuroscientist by training). 'Speech is processed in Wernicke's . . . no wait.'"[6]

Hoel notes that college science courses on neuroscience often start with the famous case of Phineas Gage, a railroad worker in the Victorian era who survived having a metal rod fly through his eye socket and out the back of his skull. This supposedly changed his personality (as Hoel mentions, the evidence for this change is somewhat overhyped), which supposedly proved that selfhood is located in the prefrontal cortex, which took the brunt of the damage from the rod.

But supposing this were true, what does it tell us about how the prefrontal cortex creates the actual experience of being Phineas Gage? Nothing at all, Hoel suggests, because location does not explain causation. "If personality had instead been located to the side of the brain, rather than the front, what would that change?" Nothing of substance: "If you ask me how a car works, and I say 'well right here is the engine, and there are the wheels, and the steering wheel, that's inside,' and so on, you'd quickly come to the conclusion that I have no idea how a car actually works."[7]

## The Permanent Anomaly

This problem was anticipated at the beginning of the modern scientific age. "It must be confessed," wrote Gottfried Leibniz in 1714, "that perception, and that which depends on it, are inexplicable by mechanical causes, that is by figures and motions."[8] Though he had seen neither an automobile engine nor an MRI machine, Leibniz saw

Hoel's point coming three centuries in advance. "Supposing there were a machine," he wrote, "so constructed as to think, feel, and have perception, it might be conceived as increased in size, while keeping the same proportions, so that one might go into it as into a mill. That being so, we should, on examining its interior, find only parts which work one upon another, and never anything by which to explain a perception."

Yet perception obviously exists. If it didn't, the perceptual you would not be reading the perceptual me reproducing the claims of the perceptual Leibniz three hundred years after the fact. So when the confident Clinton-era neuroscientists told Tom Wolfe that they had opened the brain and found no single seat of self-awareness, no organ where the mind or soul sits throbbing happily away, they were undermining their own confident materialism, not confirming it. If you can't find the source and substance of a phenomenon even when its material substrate is laid bare before you, then you haven't successfully reduced the phenomenon to that substrate or otherwise explained its origin. You've just discovered an apparent limit on your material investigation.

For centuries that limit was accepted by, indeed built into, the scientific project. Just as science excluded the possibility of supernatural agents from its search for explanations, it also tended to make a distinction between the realities of chemistry and physics, the "pieces which push one against another" and whose movements could be mapped and measured and predicted, and the mental substance of human consciousness and perception.

Like the exclusion of divine intervention, the exclusion of the subjective self was arguably useful to scientific progress, enabling increasingly detailed explanations of how all of the impersonal elements of existence interact and fit together. And it remains similarly useful to the progress of brain science today. The march through Chalmers' "easy problems" can continue because scientists aren't pausing to plumb the mysterious substance of orangeness or the unfathomability of self-awareness when they're trying to analyze how the eye and the nose transmit signals to the brain. A confident popularizer of science like Steven Pinker can write an engaging book with the title *How the Mind Works*, rattling through all manner of interesting theories before conceding, at the close, that among the problems left unexplained by his efforts are "consciousness . . . the self . . . the unified center of sentience . . . free will . . . knowledge . . . meaning . . . morality."[9] One could chuckle at this list—just a few small things to figure out!—but it actually reflects an admirable kind of practical humility, which lets the easy problems keep on getting tackled even though the hard problems continue to be baffling.

But just as the practical rule against immediate supernatural explanations degenerated into an unwarranted philosophical bias against recognizing order and design, the exclusion of subjective experience from scientific analysis has gradually created an unwarranted hope among ambitious reductionists that Leibniz was simply wrong—that the bafflement at the end of Pinker's book is only provisional, and that perception, will, reason, and selfhood itself will eventually be enfolded into the system of physical causality. And then, more recently and more crudely, this hope has curdled into a presumption that reductive physical explanations already suffice to explain subjective experience.

Thus you get the popular idea that if you've figured out where the brain seems to store the neurological data associated with a particular memory, you've explained the specific thoughts and experiences that people have when they wallow in nostalgia or relive some dreadful trauma. Or that once you can determine, say, the key hormones involved in sensitizing a new mother's brain to be especially responsive to her own newborn's face and cries, you have explained the stormy experience of motherhood itself. Or that if you've found the neuron that fires when you see a picture of the forty-second president of the United States, you've explained exactly how the idea of Bill Clinton might haunt a right-wing mind.

These are not just popular prejudices. A remarkable amount of philosophical energy has been expended trying to argue that it makes sense to explain mental states in terms of their physical correlates. But whether you read a thousand pages of that kind of writing or just a few examples, what's on offer either feels like so much humbug or a well-meaning exercise in missing the point. In the end the emperor is always naked: redescribe as you will, reduce as you may, nobody has any idea how or why the physical inputs that go into conscious experience, the stimuli from particular chemicals or light waves or exchanges between neurons, yield the actual experiences themselves.[10]

Of course consciousness exists in some kind of dynamic relationship to physical reality; nobody who's encountered alcohol or pot or caffeine doubts that the experience of selfhood can be altered by conducting chemistry experiments in your bloodstream or your brain. But all the immense progress we've made in figuring out how chemistry and biology interact in the pathways of the cerebellum has brought us no closer to answering the question of why these physical interactions yield both conscious self-awareness generally and the specific kind of experience we have. What the mother with the newborn actually feels can still only be described, one consciousness expressing itself to another consciousness, and even then only imperfectly and provisionally. It cannot be quantified or measured or dissected; it does not follow mechanically in any way we can understand from the chemical composition of oxytocin or the exchanges between maternally important neurons.[11] The gulf between the two kinds of things isn't just vast, it's infinite.

Here is how philosopher and theologian David Bentley Hart distills the "hard problem," in his florid but effective style:

> There seems to be no conceivable causal model, of the sort credible
> to modern scientific method, that could seamlessly, intelligibly
> explain to us how the electrochemistry of the brain, which is
> mechanically uniform and physically causal, could generate the
> unique, varied, and incommunicable experience of a particular

person's inner phenomenal world. The first-person perspective is not dissoluble into a third-person narrative of reality; consciousness cannot be satisfactorily reduced to physics without subtracting something. The redness of the red, red rose in my garden, as I consciously experience it while gazing at the rose in a poetic reverie, has objective existence not in the molecules or biochemical events that compose those petals, that stem, or those thorns, or that compose my synapses, my sensory apparatus, or the electrochemical reactions going on in my brain. The phenomenal experience is in my mind but has no physical presence in my brain or in the world around me; no visible "red plasm" detaches itself from the petals of the rose and nimbly slips in through my optic nerves and then across the axons of my brain, retaining its visible redness all along the way. . . . Yes, the rose is "red" because it has certain properties that reflect light in a way that is chromatically legible, so to speak, when translated through the human eyes and optic nerves and brain. But the real mystery lies on the other side of that process, entirely in the subjectivity that is the site of those impressions, and hence in their irreducibly subjective character.[12]

This is not only true but obviously true, for all that it cuts against most contemporary prejudices. Suppose that you had never seen or smelled a flower, but you possessed a perfect physical-chemical-neurological map, from start to finish, of how the scent or reflected light of the rose reached Hart's brain, how molecules and particles were translated into neural interactions. Could you ascend, from that step-by-step understanding, to anything remotely like the experience of rose-ness in Hart's consciousness? To say nothing of the experience of "poetic reverie" that follows? Or the philosophical flights or novelistic creativity that the reverie inspires in turn?

Again, you could potentially identify some of the physical states associated with these experiences—identifying heightened activity in this part of the brain when Hart spies the rose, diminished activity over there when he lapses into a meditative spell, a sudden spark over there when his consciousness begins to generate a new fantastic story (or a denunciation of his theological opponents). All of that, our science can do already to some degree, and will be able to do with increasing proficiency—perhaps even with an assist from artificial intelligence along the way. The problem, the hard problem, is that there is no measurable material correspondence between these physical states and our experiences and thoughts, no sense in which knowing more and more about the molecules or electric impulses tells you more, or really anything at all, about what it's like to be David Bentley Hart.

This doesn't prove that consciousness is "supernatural" in the sense of belonging to a different order of existence than our universe; it doesn't prove the existence of an immortal soul transcending time and space, and indeed neither Chalmers nor Hoel nor many of the scientists and philosophers who endorse the hard-problem insight are conventionally religious. But at the very least it shows, as Hoel puts it, that the science of consciousness is "pre-paradigmatic": Its practitioners are staring at an "unexplained anomaly," the strange fact of mind and self, and all their labors are just working around the edges of the anomaly, explaining inputs and making maps without any clear sense of what's going on inside.

Which is to say that after five hundred years of scientific discovery, consciousness still looks just as supernatural in the colloquial sense—meaning "super-material" or "super-physical," not just another arrangement of atoms but a distinct irreducability of some kind, acting on physical reality without being physical itself—as it did in the era of Descartes or Leibniz.

## The Magical Thinking of Emergence

Look closely, and even the attempts to explain consciousness in materialist or physicalist terms tend to tacitly concede this supernaturalism.

One such argument is that conscious experience is "emergent"—a phenomenon arising at certain levels of complexity without being reducible to that complexity's component parts. This is, again, the implicit or explicit hope of certain AI programmers—that artificial selfhood will eventually "emerge," mysteriously, from sufficiently dazzling computational complexity, in the same way that human consciousness may have emerged in some kind of relationship with our own biological complexity, our larger heads and bigger brains and more complicated neural networks relative to lower forms of life.

But showing when and where a phenomenon appears, what kind of physical substrate it requires to inhabit material reality, is not the same as showing why or how the appearance happens, let alone what the phenomenon really is. And there is no obvious analogy in other examples of so-called emergence that fits with what we are trying to explain in the case of consciousness.

To go back to the automobile example, for instance, you might say that a car's motion is "emergent"—you can't identify the phenomenon of motion with any single part of the car, with the engine or steering or the wheels alone, but you can see it when all the components are working together to produce a speeding Volkswagen.

But everything you need to understand about the car in motion is physically evident and readily explicable. As an observer you can see and feel the thing the word *motion* describes, the physical parts of the automobile yielding a physical experience.

Whereas the thing itself that emerges, supposedly, from all the neurons of the brain remains fundamentally inaccessible to everyone outside the individual's consciousness, and its workings cannot be simply described with references to the cooperating aspects of the brain. Scan or dissect as you please, there is nothing that necessarily connects my own hypothetical Bill Clinton neuron to the specific details of a column about Clinton that I might happen to be writing in my head at that particular moment. But that necessary connection does exist with the phenomenon of motion, which is physically inseparable from the turning wheels, the moving car. With our Volkswagen the emergence of motion is seamless; there is no gap that needs to be bridged. In the case of neurons and the mind, "emergence" is just another way of redescribing the gap without bridging it at all.

Or again, you might say that the novel *David Copperfield* as a thing unto itself "emerges" from the material substrate of print and paper. Or that the Boston Red Sox as a thing unto itself "emerges" from the discrete components of twenty-five human athletes, a front office, Fenway Park, a fan base, and so forth. These are both cases where the emergent thing doesn't have the kind of simple physical reality that you see in the car's motion. The novel and the team are more detached from their material substrates and yet both obviously exist.

But both enjoy that existence, crucially, within the preexisting consciousness of readers and baseball fans. Their realities emerge as subcreations of the human mind, or as transmissions between Dickens' mind and our own, meaning that their forms of emergence are not analogous to the emergence of consciousness but fundamentally dependent on its immaterial mystery for their own immaterial existence.

Put another way, a baseball franchise exists to us but it does not exist to itself. It doesn't dream or love or feel resentment, write *David Copperfield* or rage against its own mortality. If we had reason to believe that it did, if the scoreboard at Fenway suddenly blared out a soliloquy in some mysterious language, the first move of the ownership would probably be to call in a ghost hunter—or hire an exorcist.

And for good reason, because "emergence" as an explanation for consciousness is finally indistinguishable from some kind of ghostly summoning. As Thomas Nagel puts it (the emphasis is mine) in his potent antimaterialist polemic *Mind and Cosmos*:

> If emergence is the whole truth, it implies that mental states
> are present in the organism as a whole, or in its central nervous

system, without any grounding in the elements that constitute the organism, except for the physical character of those elements that permits them to be arranged in the complex form that, according to the higher-level theory, connects the physical with the mental. That such purely physical elements, when combined in a certain way, should necessarily produce a state of the whole that is not constituted out of the properties and relations of the physical parts *still seems like magic* even if the higher-order psychophysical dependencies are quite systematic.[13]

## The Illusions of Illusionism

All of this makes understandable the alternative materialist move: you declare the problem a nonproblem and do away with the magic by doing away with consciousness itself. In this theory, the thing to be explained, selfhood, is ultimately an illusion; we just are the nerves and synapses and blood vessels and olfactory bulbs, which in turn yield various complex systems of data processing and response to stimulus, to which it has proven adaptive to attach an illusion of synthesis, a false sense of a "self" presiding over the various physical mechanisms of the body and the brain.

It's easy to regard this view as simply self-refuting, despite its association with some impressive intellects—because it denies the existence not just of the thing to be explained but of the mind offering the explanation, the mind receiving it, and indeed a world in which things like "clever explanations" would make sense at all. Nagel, describing the version of illusionism advanced by the late Daniel Dennett, writes that "only a philosopher could convince himself of something so implausible"[14] and a sensible person might end the discussion there.

But even if one tries to take illusionism more seriously, the evidence cited in its favor tends to look pretty unimpressive. For obvious reasons illusionists can never prove that consciousness does not exist, so they are always looking for proof that conscious experience is at the very least extraneous, stapled on to processes that could theoretically run identically without self-awareness, thought, or choice.

A famous example, often cited, is a set of experiments originating with the neuroscientist Benjamin Libet, in which subjects were asked to move their finger and also to identify the moment at which they consciously decided to make the movement. The initial experiments seemed to show rising neural activity before the decision to move was consciously made, which was interpreted (by others, it should be noted, not Libet himself) as evidence that the unconscious brain process yielded the movement, and the conscious "choice" just trailed along, like a turn signal that comes on automatically in a car programmed to drive along a given course.

But the (many, many) cleverly designed follow-on experiments made it clear that the neural activity being measured was probably just a general preparatory activity, which showed up, for instance, in cases where subjects moved a specified finger, cases where they chose which finger to move, and cases where they simply made a silent choice between items. The measured activity didn't allow you to predict which choice or which movement; at best it predicted the likelihood of some kind of eventual decision. Further experiments managed to distinguish between this general preparatory neural activity and more specific preparation for movement, which showed up only after the conscious decision to make the movement. A 2021 paper published in *Consciousness and Cognition* concluded that after decades of research, Libet's results provided no grounds to reject the commonsensical premise that "my wanting is causally responsible for my reaching," let alone evidence that "my wanting" does not actually exist.[15]

The deeper issue, though, is that even someone who firmly believes that mental experiences like "wanting" only coincide with our actions and have no real causal role—that the conscious self is like a person in a movie theater watching events unfold on screen

and imagining they control them—has not actually replaced a supernatural understanding of consciousness so much as they have restated
it on different terms. The self in that conceit isn't really nonexistent,
it's just trapped and constantly deceived—an idea familiar from gnostic cosmology, where human souls are prisoners of their bodies, the
immaterial ensnared in flesh. Or again, the idea that your sense of free
will is an illusion or that your sense of personal identity involves an
artificial separation of an illusory "self" from the larger flow of reality
are both familiar religious claims, predestinarian or Buddhist—the
metaphysical once more stealing up on the materialist unawares. Even
the language of illusion is telling, since it naturally implies a conjuring, some mysterious act of summoning, some Titania or Oberon
making us dream that we exist—returning once again to a situation
where the supposedly materialist explanation of consciousness seems
indistinguishable from magic.

In the end, the idea that we have available some clearly more
rational or more scientific alternative to a "naively" supernatural
understanding of the mind is itself fundamentally naive. Whatever
consciousness may be, soul or mind, dream or spell, it self-evidently
has its own integrity, its own being, which is intertwined with
physical reality without being reducible to physical substances and
their interactions. We all know this, at some level, because we cannot
not know it; the attempt to refuse the knowledge is itself a manifestation of the very thing that's supposedly being refused or overthrown.
Mind cannot reduce mind; consciousness cannot explain itself away.
The soul may not be exactly as ancient religions imagined it, but
under any conceivable paradigm it will always be very much alive.

## A Key That Fits the Lock

This resilience is only the first part of the mind-based argument for
taking religion seriously. You can stop at the mystery, acknowledge

the anomaly, without necessarily being drawn toward religious explanations, let alone religious duties. You see this response, for instance, among contemporary sympathizers with "panpsychism" (Nagel, for instance, inclines in this direction), the view that consciousness is a mysterious property of the universe that may inhere somehow in almost everything, trees and rocks as well as dogs and ducks and human beings, without necessarily being proof of a higher ordering by any higher Mind.[16]

Or you can follow those materialists who are content to concede the impossibility of full reductionism, to acknowledge that our subjectivity places some permanent limit on the scientific project, while arguing that these limits are actually evidence *for* materialism—that they're what you would expect from creatures that evolved strictly through contingency and chance. If we are unable to grasp certain key features of our own existence, the origins of self-awareness above all, it's probably because we're just cosmic accidents—because of course you'd expect an entirely contingent creature to face hard limits on its self-understanding, to remain at certain levels a mystery to itself.

Meditate on this argument for a moment, though, and you may find yourself circling important questions: Why has it taken us this long to reach our limit? Why should only the inward self refuse to yield to our understanding, when the rest of the universe, supposedly equally indifferent to our existence, has opened door upon door to our investigations? Why, if human consciousness is just an illusion somehow superimposed upon our body's response to physical stimuli, has the human mind been able to penetrate so deeply into the mysteries of the cosmos, rather than having its efforts closed off early on by the constraints inherent in being just an ambitious ape?

As Nagel writes, "it is not merely the subjectivity of thought but its capacity to transcend subjectivity and discover what is objectively the case" that presents a problem for a hard materialism.[17] Some degree of human understanding, yes, can perhaps be explained by evolutionary adaptation and hominid fitness alone. A cognitive response to stimuli that enabled early *Homo sapiens* to recognize the patterns of a predator's behavior has obvious adaptive use beyond just panther dodging. Even here one might have doubts that under strictly materialist premises, such a cognitive response could ever represent a fully trustworthy form of reasoning.[18] But stipulate for the sake of argument that such an adaptation alone could, at least, grant our hominid ancestors a reliable understanding of the basic rules of physical existence.

It's much harder, though, to explain why this process has kept on working at each new level of exploration, as the practical gives way to the theoretical, the simple to the complex, the intuitive to the rather more mysterious, without any obvious evolutionary pressure forcing each new leap. "Is it credible," Nagel asks, "that selection for fitness in the prehistoric past should have fixed capacities that are effective in theoretical pursuits that were unimaginable at the time?"[19] In other words, why should capacities that evolved because we needed to hunt gazelles and avoid predators also turn out, *mirabile dictu*, to be capacities that enable us to understand the laws of physics and of chemistry, to achieve manned spaceflight, to split the atom, to condense all of human knowledge onto a tiny piece of silicon? Why should a crudely practical toolset that's helpful for African or Mesopotamian survival turn out to be so extraordinarily elastic in its applications?

Here is an imperfect analogy that might help clarify the strange coincidence involved. Suppose that as a child you developed a private language to use with your siblings or your friends—a simple set of codes, slightly more sophisticated than pig latin, with the eminently practical purpose of enabling private communication that grown-ups wouldn't understand. Let that stand for the survival-driven toolkit of our primeval ancestors.

Then much later in life, suppose you discovered that this childish system enabled you and only you to read and understand a set of ancient texts, as complex as Shakespeare and Aristotle put together, that contained all the secrets of Mayan astronomy, Greek philosophy, and Egyptian mysticism, and that you happened to discover hidden in the attic of your childhood home.

Would you just assume, *Well, I was a bright kid and putting one over on grown-ups really builds linguistic skills; no wonder I was able to read the Ancient Book of Esoteric Knowledge that just happened to be hanging around in my vicinity?*

Or would you accept the more obvious conclusion—that you were a character in a larger story, and that the book was in some sense placed there for you?

But even this analogy actually concedes too much, because at the very least we can assume that the book of secrets and the childish patois have some sort of baseline commonality, rooted in the shared structures of human language, that might (however improbably) enable the child-speak to unlock the ancient text. Whereas there is much less reason to expect that the cognitive skills required to hunt wild animals and build shelters on the African savannah would have anything to do with the toolkit required for J. Robert Oppenheimer to split the universe's fundamental particles.

We take that second link for granted because it obviously exists, because our entire civilization depends upon it. But its existence and civilization-building success just compound the extraordinary coincidences discussed in the last chapter. It isn't merely that the universe appears improbably fine-tuned to enable our existence. It's that our own consciousness seems improbably capable when it comes to discovering that fine-tuning, like a key fitted to a lock.

Even the strongest nonreligious explanation for cosmological fine-tuning, the multiverse theory, only makes the fit between our consciousness and material reality seem that much more improbable. Under its conceit we are not just asked to believe in a near-infinite expanse of universes, all invisible to us. We must also accept that the utterly contingent, crudely evolved and cosmically insignificant competencies of one apelike species in the backwater of one cosmos among trillions would somehow enable that same ape to discern the existence of all those invisible universes—to grasp with godlike capacities of reason and induction and imagination the endless realities that are allegedly necessary to exclude the possibility of a single Creator God.

This isn't just a challenge for materialists. It's also a challenge for the nonreligious panpsychist, the believer in mind or consciousness as an invisible but universal property that yields strange and inaccessible-to-us forms of subjectivity up and down the tree of life. Allowing that this might be true, that the dryads might be with us after all, why does *our* variety of subjectivity yield not just subjective awareness but actual understanding? Why is selfhood in our case linked to such powerful forms of reason, logic, and understanding? What connects our direct experience of the redness of the rose or the taste of red wine to our ability to grasp the related complexities of biology and chemistry? The simplest answer is still the religious one: That the "I Am" of consciousness doesn't just coexist with matter but precedes and shapes and organizes it, and human minds are unusually good at understanding the universe because we are further up the hierarchy than the animal minds with which we share the world, closer to the higher Mind or minds that preside and shape and supervise.

Seen in this light, the habit of thinking that regards scientific progress as perpetually diminishing the reasonability of religion has things backward. The idea that the cosmos was intended, that mind is more fundamental than matter, that our minds in particular have a special relationship to the physical world and its originating Cause—all of these ideas have had their plausibility strengthened, not weakened, by centuries of scientific success. We have much better evidence for the proposition that the universe was made with human beings in mind, given our extraordinary success in discovery and interpretation, than ancient or medieval peoples ever did. We have gone far deeper than our more religious ancestors into the secret book in the attic, translated chapter upon chapter, passage after passage—to the point where we simply take for granted the strange fact that so much of it is written in a language we can understand, as though its authors knew that we'd be opening its pages one day.

Thus the entire scientific enterprise, so long as it retains confidence in itself, necessarily also retains a certain kind of religious attitude toward the universe, no matter how far it strays from actual belief. Or as Hart puts it, in doing the work of science "we assume that the human mind can be a true mirror of objective reality because we assume that objective reality is already a mirror of mind."[20] And the repeated vindication of those conjoined assumptions, across so many centuries of human advancement, fits together with the strange realities all those advancements have discovered—above all, the reality that the cosmos only looks indifferent until you open up the hood, and then all its mechanisms and calibrations turn out to point in one direction, toward making *us* possible, the readers that the book of nature was awaiting all along.

So the long arc of science, which initially seems to bend away from religion by undermining certain specific scriptural or dogmatic claims, ultimately bends back by confirming humanity's unique position in a universe strangely suited to both our bodies and our minds.

But surely, at least, science has excluded some element of the old case for religion's reasonability—all the stuff of supernatural events, invisible beings, strange revelations and mystical encounters; all the signs invoked to claim not just a higher purpose for the cosmos but a personal, active, interventionist sort of God. One may doubt that science has fully undermined some sort of general religious attitude, some deist faith in a grand design. But surely it has undermined magic and miracle; surely one cannot deny the modern disenchantment of the world.

The next chapter does deny it. Read on.

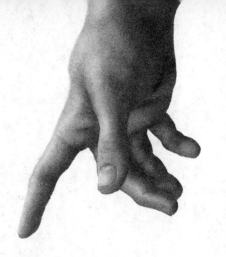

3

# The Myth of
# Disenchantment

I n the early 2010s, the fiancée of a prominent American writer moved from her native Germany to California. Among the heirlooms she brought with her was a broken 1978 Philips transistor radio, a gift from her deceased grandfather, Walter. She had been raised by a single mother, and Walter, a music lover, had played the paternal role in her life until his death when she was sixteen. The radio had been dead since then as well, and the woman's American fiancé, understanding its significance, tried to get it working—new batteries, new connections, even what he jokingly called the "percussive maintenance" of smacking it hard from different angles. Nothing worked, and the couple placed it in the back of a bedroom drawer and forgot about it.

Flash-forward to their wedding day: an exchange of signatures in a Beverly Hills courthouse, an exchange of rings at home with a crowd of family and friends. But most of the crowd was there for the American groom, and his bride, feeling isolated and homesick and wishing that her grandfather had been there to give her away, asked the groom to take her away from the crowd, into the back of the house, where they could hear music playing. Mysterious music, since nothing was turned on—not computers or stereos or iPhones or any other system—and yet the music was a love song, the kind you would play for the first dance at a wedding.

Finally they found the source: the grandfather's broken radio, in the back of the desk drawer, working again for the first time in decades, spilling romantic music into their Californian home. A relative told them that she had heard it begin playing just as the wedding ceremony started. It played all that night, switching from love songs to classical music; the next morning it was dead once more, and it never worked again.

In his famous case for presumptively disbelieving in all miracles, the Scottish philosopher David Hume argued that with any supposed witness to the supernatural, however credible they might otherwise appear, it's always more likely that they are either credulous or lying than that a supernatural event has actually occurred. The Hume rule is set up to be universally discrediting, but if you were looking for someone who would come closest to passing its exacting test, someone with every incentive not to lie or be deceived, the source for this touching not-quite-ghost story is an unusually good candidate. The bridegroom in the story, the American writer, happens to be Michael Shermer, proud atheist, editor of *Skeptical Inquirer* magazine, and a man who has spent his entire professional career trying to debunk the supernatural.[1]

The mysterious radio didn't make him a religious believer, but it clearly made an impression. He's told and retold the story in different settings ever since, and his speculative explanations are themselves revealing—but we'll come back around to that. For now, Shermer's radio can stand as a condensed symbol for this chapter's theme: the myth of a disenchanted modern world, the persistence of supernatural happenings, and the credible reasons to think that material reality isn't a closed system but one zone, and a porous zone at that, within a larger whole.

## The Resilience of the Supernatural

The idea that modernity means the death of miracle and magic is shared by writers who welcome disenchantment and those who lament its progress. From confident twenty-first-century champions of Enlightenment to romantic poets pining for a glimpse of Hermes, from antisupernaturalist New Atheists to woo-besotted New Agers, the story is always the same: Once human beings inhabited a supernatural-infused cosmos, saw divinity in every tree and waterfall, lived under the influence of angels and demons, gods and stars and spirits. Now we inhabit a society defined by reason, science, and calculation, a natural world drained of metaphysical significance, with selves buffered against the mystical and mythological.

Maybe this is a story of progress—modernity as the realm of light, reason's candle burning amid the demon-haunted dark. Or maybe this is a tale of loss, of capacities suppressed and knowledge given up, of eyes closed that we should open once again. Or maybe it's just an ambiguous story, with gains and losses and trade-offs. But most people debating the issue assume that disenchantment in some form was achieved.

And for good reason, because in the realm that most writers and intellectuals and academics inhabit, the realm of Official Knowledge, disenchantment reigns supreme. Almost all "knowledge production" in the modern world, whether it takes place in universities or bureaucracies or the respectable portions of the media, is informed by a practical atheism, a presumption that you must always analyze human life in scientific or at least social-scientific terms, keeping God or the supernatural safely off the stage. Disenchantment in this specific sense is a modern consensus, an intellectual default, even for the sort of academics and journalists and Wikipedia editors who might show up for church on Sunday, take a glance at their horoscope, light a candle or burn a little incense, or otherwise personally defect from disenchanted premises.

But disenchantment as a description of human experience is a false paradigm, fundamentally mistaken about what it's like to be a human being in the modern world. When intellectuals stopped taking mystical experiences seriously, actual human beings kept on having the experiences. When Official Knowledge ruled out the supernatural, in ordinary life it kept on breaking in. Science supplanted prayer, for good reason, as the primary means of seeking healing, but people kept on reporting that they'd been healed by intercessory prayer. The afterlife ceased to be a respectable subject for theory and argument, but people kept on having visions, seeing ghosts, and reporting strange experiences at the threshold of death at a pace not obviously different—or in the case of near-death experiences, at higher rates—than in the more religious past.

The resilience of enchantment is not merely a matter of people continuing to believe in gods or angels or an afterlife, holding on to faith in defiance of the evidence and then interpreting peculiar events in light of that defiant faith. Modern human beings continue to have the kinds of experiences that are fundamental to religion even when they have no religious expectations or beliefs, give spiritual possibilities no credence in advance, and indeed believe firmly themselves in the idea of disenchantment—right up until the moment they hit death's threshold, or hear music wafting from a broken radio, or feel the numinous descend on them unbidden. You can be the most hardened of materialists and still find yourself in "a furious encounter with a living substance that was coming at me through all things at once," to quote one of the descriptions of mystical experience in *Living with a Wild God*, Barbara Ehrenreich's memoir of being an inveterate skeptic graced with intense brushes with the Absolute.[2] You can believe that nothing, absolutely nothing, awaits you after death and come back from the operating table transformed, or at least badly shaken in your nonbelief. You can disbelieve entirely in ghosts and the demonic and find yourself, to your shock, dealing with something in your life that has you calling up an exorcist.

This was not how disenchantment's prophets expected secular modernity to work. Here is Hume in his eighteenth-century essay, offering one of his several reasons for disbelief: "It forms a strong presumption against all supernatural and miraculous relations, that they are observed chiefly to abound among ignorant and barbarous nations; or if a civilized people has ever given admission to any of them, that people will be found to have received them from ignorant and barbarous ancestors, who transmitted them with that inviolable sanction and authority, which always attend received opinions."[3] This idea retains a certain currency in anthropological theories of religion, where religious belief is supposed to arise from a mixture of psychological habits, political needs, and what Hume in the same essay calls "the usual propensity of mankind towards the marvellous," which then transmute deliberate lies and misty legends into pseudohistory and supernatural dogma. But the two hundred years and more of very modern history since Hume suggest a different story, in which a crucial taproot of religious belief is simply the brute fact of religious experience—a constant in human affairs, under "civilized" as well as "barbarous" conditions, whose mysteries constantly cry out for interpretation and yield new religious systems organically when old ones seem to fade.

To be fair, Hume does not claim that mysticism will simply disappear under secular conditions; the impulse to believe against the evidence can "receive a check from sense and learning," but "it can never be thoroughly extirpated from human nature." And it's also fair for skeptics to note that Hume was especially concerned with some of the big miracles of the Bible, and the last two hundred years have yielded no miracles on the scale of the parting of the Red Sea. (Though certain modern episodes have at least a biblical flavor, as in the so-called Miracle of the Sun in Fátima, Portugal, in 1918, when in fulfillment of promises supposedly made by the Virgin Mary to three children the sun appeared to dance before tens of thousands of witnesses.)

But the Humean account clearly implies that as religion loses its institutional power, as "received opinion" turns from credulity to skepticism, the marvelous should likewise cease to "abound" in anything like its prior form. Yet many forms of supernatural visitation, of the sort that a confident eighteenth-century analysis would confine to barbarous antiquity, have endured or reappeared in the most high-tech and scientifically minded societies. The wildness of frontier revivalism, the spiritualist experiments of the Victorian era, the return of New Testament tongues-speaking to early-twentieth-century Los Angeles (and thence to the world), the interest in near-death experiences that accelerated with the psychologist Raymond

Moody's research in the 1960s, the mysterious encounters bundled under the UFO phenomenon—in each of these cases and more, you see "marvels" with ancient lineages resurfacing in new forms under supposedly disenchanted conditions.

In some instances, to be sure, these revivals provide their own grist for Humean cynicism. No doubt the philosopher would approve of the portrayal of the Mormon prophet Joseph Smith as an all-American huckster in Broadway's *The Book of Mormon*. And the entire history of L. Ron Hubbard Scientology feels like it belongs in an Enlightenment skeptic's tract about mystical belief as an authoritarian con.

But in modernity we consistently see mystical experience as an organic phenomenon that *precedes* attempts to vest it with formal authority or enforce belief via social pressure, rather than an inheritance of myth and legend received indirectly and accepted out of a desire to go along with the social herd.

For instance, while hucksters and con men have certainly fastened onto the culture of belief that's grown up around supposed alien abductions, from the first these visitations have been notable for not fitting into any "received opinion," for occupying a weird terrain between the spiritual and scientific, for generating a multiplicity of theories but no definitive dogma. As the religious studies professor Diana Pasulka has argued, you can see in UFO culture a kind of protoreligion, in which the enchanted experience is the primary and unifying thing, and various attempts to create a theology or ufology come jostling afterward.[4]

Likewise in modernity, you can find countless phony mediums cashing in on "readings" of their clients' futures, but also a wide realm of people experiencing psychic-seeming flashes as unbidden aspects of their everyday life, unconnected to any metaphysical architecture or pecuniary advantage. For instance, few of the characters in *The Premonitions Bureau*, Sam Knight's 2022 book about the psychiatrist John Barker's attempt to study psychic experiences in mid-twentieth-century Britain, come across as participants in some cynical fraud or culturally rooted mass delusion. They're just people having outlying experiences that surprise and persist despite their secular milieu.[5]

Then in the more dramatic case of near-death experiences, a form of supernatural-seeming encounter has been discovered more fully in the modern era than was possible before. Not that there hadn't been near-death experiences in the premodern past, but so many more people are now successfully resuscitated that we can gather far more data on these experiences' frequency and consistency (and, of course, their general strangeness). Again, within the range of accounts, there are clearly pious exaggerations and hucksters building castles in the air. But most people who have these experiences aren't selling books or trying to defend a preexisting faith; indeed, there is no noticeable correlation between formal religious belief or faith in an afterlife and a near-death brush with the numinous, and when Moody began his research many of his subjects were embarrassed to talk about their experiences at all, since they assumed that doctors and psychologists would sneer at them.

That embarrassment is itself a key feature of our times. Yes, there is some natural human eagerness to believe in the supernatural, some persistent fascination with the marvelous or eerie. But as Official Knowledge has marginalized the mystical, that eagerness coexists with the opposite sort of pressure—to dismiss supernatural experiences, even one's own supernatural experiences, lest one appear deluded or disreputable. And this, in turn, leads many people to underestimate the scale and scope of weird happenings in the world, to assume that these things are more exceptional than they actually appear to be.

Yet even if people are too personally secularized or disenchanted to expect them, even if Official Knowledge gives them no "sanction and authority," the experiences keep coming, and the wisest heirs of Hume no longer expect religious experience to diminish automatically as religious institutions and traditions lose power and prestige. Instead the brightest materialists acknowledge mysticism's permanence, even sometimes concede that such experiences can run wild in the absence of institutional religion. They simply deny that they have a correlative "out there" in the numinous, insisting that we just need to look for biochemical or psychological explanations instead.

But before we consider those explanations, it's important to stress that just the quest for, say, the neurobiology of mystical experience is itself a retreat—a climb-down from the stronger position that made almost all supernaturalism out to be a matter of official lies, myth-making, and wishful thinking.

If spiritual experiences had actually diminished or disappeared under the official rule of disenchantment, it would have been a powerful case for the skeptical perspective: *Look, once the authorities stop embracing these stories, once the power of ecclesial authority stops encouraging them, people stop claiming or pretending to experience them.*

But nothing like that appears to be the case. The nineteenth century was more scientifically advanced than Hume's eighteenth century but also more shot through with mysticism and revivalism. The late-twentieth-century decline of institutional religion in America has had no effect on the share of Americans who report supernatural experiences; indeed, by some measures those reports have notably increased.

This means that we have proof of the resilience of spiritual experience under secular conditions that our ancestors inevitably lacked—and thus better reasons than in Hume's era to believe that these experiences reflect something more than fantasy.

## The Varieties of Spiritual Experience

But let's step back. By "these experiences," what exactly do we mean? Many different things, certainly, but within the range of spiritual experiences several categories can be usefully discussed.[6]

The first is what you might call the generic mystical experience—
"generic" not because it is boring or predictable but because it seems
to be most commonplace and the most readily accessible through
certain kinds of spiritual technique, common to religious traditions
in both the East and West. This is an experience in which the self's
relationship to reality undergoes a dramatic transformation, and some
deeper pattern of reality is apparently revealed. The revelation may
take the form of a sense of oneness with the universe, of dissolving
boundaries between the self and the world, of interconnection rather
than separation within creation, with the ego and the individual personality seemingly evaporating. Or it may involve what the scholar
of comparative religion R. C. Zaehner describes as "not the loss of
personality," the self dissolving into nature, "but rather the *realization of personality* . . . in isolation from all that is other than itself."[7]
If the first kind of experience is all about a sense of interdependence
within creation, of being one with the entire world, the second kind
of experience often feels like a revelation of the soul's absolute suffi-
ciency, its independence from its mortal flesh, its immortality.

Both aspects of this generic mysticism are often associated with a
sense of universal love, cosmic glory, a version of Julian of Norwich's
admonition that "all will be well and all will be well and all manner
of thing will be well." But neither necessarily feels like an encounter
with another being or Person, angelic or divine. Which is why even
though such experiences are probably most common among religious
practitioners, meditating and praying monks and nuns especially—
and most predictable and amenable to study in that context—when
they fall unbidden on normal human beings they are not necessarily
spurs to formal religious conversion or newfound theological belief.

Instead they might be associated with artistic or intellectual
epiphanies. Zaehner, for instance, finds examples of the one-with-
nature experience in Alfred Tennyson and the immortal-self experience in Marcel Proust that he argues match up well with Indian
mystical traditions. In his autobiography the famous atheist Bertrand

Russell cited a fleeting five-minute experience in his youth, a strange "mystic illumination" of universal love and brotherhood, as a shaping influence on his entire life and career; "something of what I thought I saw in that moment has remained with me always."[8] It's in this kind of spirit that the generic sort of experiences are often sought out nowadays, through meditative discipline or certain pharmacological interventions, by people who take it for granted that they are essentially self-revelatory rather than an opening to God or to the gods. (The New Atheist turned meditation evangelist Sam Harris offers one of the more prominent examples of this tendency.)

In this they differ from the second kind of mystical experience in our taxonomy, which involves a sense of encounter with something absolute and absolutely other. The first kind of experience can turn into the second kind; the line I'm drawing is hardly a clean one, but you see a definite difference when that transition happens, and the person having the experience is left with no doubt that Something is looking at them or pressing into and through them. Here is one example, taken from the vignettes in William James's *Varieties of Religious Experience* (to which all taxonomies of mystical experience are indebted): "All at once I felt the presence of God—I tell of the thing just as I was conscious of it—as if his goodness and his power were penetrating me altogether . . . I think it well to add that in this ecstasy of mine God had neither form, color, odor, nor taste . . . God was present, though invisible, he fell under no one of my senses, yet my consciousness perceived him."[9]

In Ehrenreich's memoir, you see the progression; she has unexpected mystical experiences that resemble the generic sense of mystical union with the cosmos, but then eventually she experiences an escalation and a personalization: "Something poured into me and I poured out into it. This was not the passive beatific merger with 'the All,' as promised by the Eastern mystics. It was a furious encounter with a living substance that was coming at me through all things at once, and one reason for the terrible wordlessness of the experience is that you cannot observe fire really closely without becoming part of it."[10]

A final example, from the experience of a Yale-educated writer at a charismatic healing service in 1980s Connecticut:

> It just came into me with a roar, and clamped onto me, like a thousand volts, or like one of those machines they use to start someone's heart on the operating table. It clamped onto both sides of my face, and over my thyroid, and gripped my arms down into my hands that were still hovering over my waist and vibrating. But I was vibrating in many other places, too, by this point, and I couldn't breathe right because my diaphragm was really tight where this power was pouring into me, and my stomach was quaking, up and down. . . .
>
> In my whole life, I had only had encounters with other people, and suddenly it was as if I were alone with God, or his Spirit, and frankly, I had no idea how to respond. I remember the name Lazarus flashing into my mind, and the incredible thought: *This is a power that could raise the dead.*[11]

The person experiencing the mystical experience in the last example, I should note, is my own mother. And just in the language she uses you can see the important role that culture plays in shaping the interpretation of religious experience. She and Ehrenreich are having very similar encounters, both unexpected and dramatic, but in her case the mediating force of the charismatic-Christian setting and her own Protestant background brings the New Testament immediately to mind and makes her assume that this is the God of her upbringing, the Holy Spirit in the Christian Trinity. Whereas Ehrenreich, raised by resolutely irreligious parents and encountering this "living substance" entirely outside the parameters of institutional religion, interprets it as a strange "Wild God" that's essentially different from the God of the Bible or the Torah or the Qur'an.

Thus her experience is transformative without being a conversion story. This seems to be a common way enchantment operates under secular conditions. People have the same kinds of experiences they once had in a more religious age; the bolt from the blue keeps falling when you least expect it. But rather than having a conceptual framework in which the experience immediately makes sense, it becomes a mysterious signifier, to be interpreted through a purely personal framework or—as in many such cases—not interpreted at all.

Here one could argue that the more secular atmosphere of modernity gets us closer to the raw substrate of the supernatural, to some universal human experience whose interpretation is normally conditioned by cultural and religious expectations.

If those expectations matter for the kind of encounter just described, they definitely matter for the third category of mystical experience, in which the supernatural condenses to a person, a particular being, a face, words. In these cases the sense of otherness doesn't go away; these are still encounters with the numinous, unsettling and eerie or just seemingly impossible in their nature and effects. But what's experienced is made manifest in a singular figure, a personality or group of personalities, a voice giving instructions, not just a harrowing or joyful experience of divinity or mystery.

A vision of Jesus or Krishna would fall into this category; so would the innumerable encounters with gods and saints and angels, departed relatives and the Virgin Mary; so would the external voice speaking to you suddenly at some crucial moment in your life. For many people these are fleeting, even once-in-a-lifetime experiences; for some they are more frequent; for a very few they feel constant, everyday. Some communities think they can be cultivated, from charismatic Christians who believe they can train themselves to distinguish God's voice within their own internal monologues to spiritualists who think that latent psychic powers can be trained and honed. In other cases they're experienced as a burden, an imposition, even a hostile takeover.

But the most normal pattern is for such visitations to come suddenly and then depart once some seeming purpose has been served. Sometimes this is moral or psychological purpose; sometimes it's a conversion or reversion. And sometimes it's a specific physical purpose, as in a famous case report from the *British Medical Journal*, in which a woman with no history of mental disturbances suddenly began heard voices instructing her (in an apologetic tone, "I know it must be shocking for you to hear me speaking to you like this . . .") to get a brain scan for a tumor. There was no medical indication for such a scan, and her doctor put her on antipsychotic medication instead, but the voices persisted and eventually the doctor was persuaded to give her a scan simply for reassurance purposes. Naturally a tumor was discovered, an operation took place, and when she recovered consciousness she heard the voices say, "We are pleased to have helped you. Goodbye." She never heard them again.[12]

In this case the patient experienced the voices as just that, voices, but usually when the supernatural is personified some more specific identity is attached. And this is where the cultural filter seems crucially important: You are more likely to have a vision of a saint if you're raised Catholic, of Jesus if you're raised evangelical, of a Hindu god if you're raised Hindu, to see an ancestral spirit in East Asian contexts where ancestor veneration is more important than in the monotheistic West. This is a pattern rather than a universal rule; there are cases of religious conversions in which, say, a non-Christian has visions of a mysterious figure whom they eventually realize is Jesus or the Virgin Mary or Saint Michael, and of course people outside of East Asia experience mysterious encounters with their relatives and ancestors. But in the aggregate, one's cultural matrix seems to take similar kinds of experiences and particularize them—with a vision of Krishna in one part of the world resembling a vision of Jesus in another, or a message from a small-g god in ancient Greece or modern India resembling an angelic visitation in early modern Europe. That framing assumes that the mind is doing the particularizing; the alternative take would be that when divinity wants to speak with you directly, it usually takes the form that you're already most likely to revere.

It's also important to stress that reverence and holy fear are not the only spiritual emotions; people also frequently experience unsettlement, anxiety, and terror, where the encounter seems malign or hostile or demonic. In these cases, there is arguably less cross-cultural variation. The specific theology of hell differs across religions, but in their practical effects demons are demons are demons, their behavior reasonably similar in both polytheistic and monotheistic systems, in Asian and European contexts. And these experiences, too, show no signs of disappearing under supposedly disenchanted conditions: demand for exorcisms in the United States has risen with traditional religion's recent ebb, a notable minority of near-death experiences are basically hellish in their details, and experimenters on the psychedelic fringe regularly report brushes with malign or threatening entities that any traditional Christian or Buddhist would recognize as devilish.[13]

We see more cross-cultural variation in the ambiguous territory between the holy and the diabolical, inhabited by those spirits that seem more neutral toward human beings, more inclined to bargains, abductions, practical jokes. These may appear as trickster gods in one context, as elves or fairies in another—and in our times, perhaps, as extraterrestrials captaining mysterious UFOs.

## The Disreputability Problem

Whether they're perceived as alien abductions or angelic visitations, the prompting of a god or the voice of God Himself, these kind of specific encounters are much more disreputable, from the perspective of Official Knowledge, than the more generic kinds of mystical experience. The experience of oneness with the universe can be folded without too much difficulty into a purely material account of human consciousness, especially insofar as some of its physiological correlates can be isolated by laboratory specialists in the brains of spiritual practitioners. (Though why it comes unbidden to non-practitioners is a bit more obscure.) The sense of invasive Otherness described by Ehrenreich or James's subject or my mother is harder to explain, but its very mystery, the fact that it often seems beyond the descriptive capacities of the person experiencing it, ends up being reassuring to the materialist. Mystery is what you'd expect from a misfiring nervous system, a brain confused by its sensory inputs.

The more concrete kind of experience, on the other hand, forces the skeptic to choose between lucid hallucination and deliberate deception, with the difficulty often being that these experiences befall people who show no evidence of being prone to either delusion or mendacity. ("Hallucinations of the sane" was the useful phrase of a nineteenth-century investigator of people visited by their departed loved ones.[14]) This yields a characteristic pattern where an expert or writer takes up the study of a certain kind of paranormal experience out of academic or journalistic curiosity and ends up convinced that something real is going on. But rather than persuading other experts to take an interest themselves, the supernatural-curious colleague gets quickly written out of polite academic society, because everybody knows that this kind of experience can't possibly correlate with something real outside the mind.

The Harvard professor of psychiatry John Mack's work with alleged UFO abductees is a famous example; he was drawn into the subject accidentally, on a friend's prompting, but ended up so disreputably convinced that something real had happened to his subjects that there was an attempt to get his tenure stripped. But there are many such cases in the backwaters of academia and the byways of journalism: people who learned a little bit too much about near-death experiences or hauntings or psychic premonitions or some other peculiar subject, and whose studies no longer fit the templates of the Official Knowledge generation. It's very hard to maintain the neutral study of mystical experience. You're either in too deep to be considered trustworthy, or you probably don't know much about the subject and assume that there's nothing interesting there at all.

This problem of the putatively neutral observer tilting toward belief goes all the way back to William James himself, who reluctantly, oh so reluctantly, allowed at the end of *Varieties of Religious Experience* that he believed in the authenticity of mystical experience himself. From a religious perspective, the predictability of this tilt offers a partial answer to the skeptical complaint that intense religious experience is either too rare to be credible, or else too concentrated among people who already believed religious dogmas to be treated as dispassionate testimony. In fact, even under our contemporary "secular" conditions it remains the case that if you go looking for spiritual experience with any kind of open mind— and by this I mean not just attending church services or throwing up occasional prayers but actually seeking out unusual people and places and practices, actively participating in their rituals, opening yourself as you would to any other aspect of human experience that you don't initially understand—then you are very likely to find what you are looking for.

Not everyone will have a personal mystical experience. Some people clearly have some kind of aptitude for spiritual communion, as others have an aptitude for living entirely inside the material world. But the secular reader might be surprised at how many seemingly well-defended materialists only seem that way because they've been reared and educated without any encounter with religion. My mother, I can testify, dragged a number of her secular friends to charismatic healing services after her own mystical experience, and more of them had extremely weird experiences than their liberal-rationalist priors would lead you to expect. Meanwhile I did *not* have those experiences, despite Christian belief and the suggestibility of youth—but like certain scholars of the arcane and impossible, what I saw just by looking was enough to leave me with a very different view of reality than the average newspaper columnist.

Of course even seeing and experiencing isn't always believing, and belief in the reality of a specific experience doesn't compel belief in how those experiences are packaged or interpreted. (Among my parents' skeptical friends, the reaction to a wild charismatic encounter was often similar to Barbara Ehrenreich's response to her brushes with the supernatural—that these were weird, trippy, mind-opening, maybe even proof of God's existence in some way, but hardly a reason to convert to Christianity.) Nor does every quest for spiritual experience have a happy ending. You may find what you're looking for and come away haunted and oppressed, because some of the spirits most eager to be summoned may not have your good in mind.

But a famous claim about God's availability, "Ask, and it will be given to you; seek, and you will find; knock, and it will be opened to you,"[15] is still a pretty good rule under modern conditions, so long as you don't mind the crankish reputation that you'll acquire if you report on what you've found. Indeed this holds even for those rare students of spiritual experience who maintain the most rigorous neutrality, the most scrupulous balance between taking the mystical seriously but never committing to supernatural explanations.

The best exemplar of this balancing act is Stanford anthropologist and psychologist Tanya Luhrmann, who has embedded in communities committed to mystical belief, from neo-pagans to charismatic Christians, and sought to understand how their practices generate experiences that match their world-pictures and affirm them in their beliefs. Her writings are unique in that the believer can read them as vindication of the points I've just made—that the combination of spiritual talent, perseverance, and embeddedness in a religious community delivers intense spiritual experiences much more reliably than a skeptic might expect. But meanwhile the skeptic can read them and assume that she's describing imagined worlds, imagined experiences, the power of the human mind to generate what it wants to hear or see—including in those passages where she acknowledges that participating with her subjects yielded spiritual experiences for her as well.

Or rather the skeptic can mostly read her work that way. But even Luhrmann is given experiences that break the skeptic's frame—like this moment, from early in her anthropological career:

> I was sitting in a commuter train to London the first time I felt supernatural power rip through me. I was 23, and one year into my graduate training in anthropology. I had decided to do my fieldwork among educated white Britons who practiced what they called magic. I thought of the topic as a clever twist on more traditional anthropological study of strange "native" customs.
>
> I was on my way to meet some of the magicians, and I had ridden my bike to the station with trepidation and excitement. On the train, as the sheep-dotted countryside rolled by, I was reading a book by a man they called an "adept"—someone they regarded as deeply knowledgeable and powerful.
>
> The book's language was dense and abstract, and my mind kept slipping as I struggled to grasp what he was talking about. The text spoke of the Holy Spirit and Tibetan masters and an ancient system of Judaic mysticism called kabbalah. The author wrote that all these were just names for forces that flowed from a higher spiritual reality into this one, through the vehicle of the trained mind. And as I strained to imagine what the author thought it would be like to be that vehicle, I began to feel power in my veins—to really feel it, not to imagine it. I grew hot. I became completely alert, more awake than I usually am, and I felt so alive. It seemed that power coursed through me like water through a chute. I wanted to sing. And then wisps of smoke came out of my backpack, in which I had tossed my bicycle lights. One of them was melting.[16]

## From Mystical to Miracle

This brings us to the fourth kind of mystical experience, from the point of view of Official Knowledge the most disreputable of all— the kind of mystical experience that actually has apparent effects in material reality, whether miraculous, uncanny, or simply really, really weird. The melting batteries belong to the last category, as does Michael Shermer's radio. So do some of the more intense stories associated with exorcisms, hauntings, poltergeists. So do the insistent claims of folk religion—e.g., that the saint's statue really wept—and some of the claims of bodily effects or poltergeist-like sequelae to UFO encounters. So do the historical claims, modern as well as ancient, that Official Knowledge rules out as legends or delusions despite their evidentiary basis—like the Miracle of the Sun in the disenchanted year of 1917, or the detailed accounts from multiple witnesses attesting to levitating saints across the sixteenth and seventeenth century, catalogued in the Yale historian Carlos Eire's recent book *They Flew*.[17]

The most consistently attested example of the mystical interacting with the material is the phenomenon of miraculous healings— seemingly impossible recovery after intercessory prayer. That attestation takes many different forms, with the simplest being the share of contemporary people who claim to have experienced or witnessed a miraculous healing. It's about a third of Americans, according to survey data, with higher shares in other regions of the world, meaning that hundreds of millions of people around the globe believe that they witnessed a concrete supernatural intervention in their lives.[18]

No skeptic would or should take all those myriad claims at face value. But if you try to drill down to the kind of experiences people are talking about in these surveys (as the evangelical scholar Craig Keener attempts to do, for instance, in his two-volume, twelve-hundred-page work *Miracles: The Credibility of the New Testament Accounts*), they are often much more extreme and dramatic, much closer to the kind of accounts in, say, the gospel of Mark, than someone praying to get better from a flu or injury and then recovering.[19] Which makes them worth citing, at the very least, as further proof of how poorly Humean presuppositions about modernity have fared, how normal and commonplace extreme forms of religious experience remain.

There also happens to be a systematizing institution that's extremely interested in the phenomenon, collecting anecdotes, investigating medical case histories, soliciting physician testimony, and genuinely trying to go as far as you can in ruling out natural explanations for the healings. That would be the Catholic Church, whose process of saint-making depends on scientific investigation and a process of exclusion. To qualify for consideration, the illness that's been allegedly cured by a saint's intercession must be incurable, it must be documented by medical authorities, it must be organic to the body and not psychiatric, there must be no treatment that might account for the shift, the healing must be sudden and immediate, and there must be a full recovery.

Obviously this attempt at rigor still leaves plenty of room to doubt the church's neutrality and judgment. But the scientific aspects of the process have clearly become more rigorous as scientific knowledge has advanced, medical cures have become much more effective, and diseases have become better understood. (To pluck a very recent example, during the 2023 World Youth Day pilgrimage to Fátima in Portugal a teenager reported being suddenly healed of a condition that had rendered her nearly blind, a potential miracle that could never become an officially approved miracle because the underlying condition has been known to spontaneously resolve.) So if you turn back to Hume's confident depiction of miracles as the fruits of credulity and legend, you might expect that past a certain threshold of scientific understanding the Catholic Church would face a crisis of miracles, a fatal shortfall of the necessary healings required to make its saints—because almost every seeming healing would turn out, upon careful medical examination, to have some plausible material explanation.

Perhaps that threshold awaits us in the future, but the last fifty years have seen instead a dramatic acceleration in saint-making, driven especially by Pope John Paul II's enthusiasm for canonization. It's true that as part of this enthusiasm the Polish pope dropped the threshold for confirmed miracles from three per saint to merely two—but that relaxation of standards was more than offset statistically by the sheer number of canonizations, such that the Vatican has approved hundreds and hundreds more miracles under the eye of secular medical authorities and a skeptical mass media than it did in Hume's era, or for that matter in the medical obscurity of the Middle Ages.[20]

Just to be clear about the kinds of miraculous-seeming events we're talking about here, I want to offer an example that isn't from the church's saint-making process, but has the advantage of being written up as a medical case report. It involves an infant who began vomiting uncontrollably at two weeks of age and was diagnosed with gastroparesis, a chronic, lifelong condition that involves nausea, chest and abdominal pain, and vomiting. One of the recommended treatments is a surgical insertion of a feeding tube, which this patient received as a child, and lived most of his life completely dependent on the tube for eating and drinking. He received no other notable medical treatment. At twenty-three, his condition unchanged, he attended a Pentecostalist healing service, led by a preacher with a reputation for healing prayer. At which point the following ensued:

> After the sermon, the evangelist talked to the boy and they "compared battle-scars", as both went through several surgeries, developing an instant comradery. He asked the whole family to gather, and he led a time of PIP (laying hands upon the boy's shoulders). The patient doesn't recall how long the PIP intervention took but

mentions that he was prayed for only once. The intercessor prayed that, in the name of Jesus, the boy's stomach be healed. He commanded the healing in the authority and power of Jesus. He made a point of indicating that he had no power or authority to heal, but only with the authority of Jesus Christ, he could command the healing. Halfway through the prayer the boy recalls a shock starting from his right shoulder going down in a diagonal angle across his abdomen and described it as a pulsating and electrical sensation. It surprised the boy, and he reports that he also experienced some pain at the time of the shock. Despite the discomfort, they continued to pray a while longer. The experience is consistent with prior accounts, from scholarly practitioners, who have noted that "About 50 percent of people who are healed feel something . . . heat, electricity, tingling, coolness, pain going away." . . .

That night after prayer, he ate a meal for the first time without any complications . . . his intolerance to oral feedings was completely resolved. He was able to tolerate oral feedings and was completely taken off of the j-tube feedings one month after the PIP experience. The patient's pediatric gastroenterologist, who was his primary care physician for sixteen years, described his case as difficult to explain.[21]

As with the persistence of mystical experience generally, we now take it for granted that these kinds of experiences continue happening, whatever the underlying explanation may be. But this persistence was not at all predictable when the age of modern science dawned. If spontaneous prayer-associated healings had all but evaporated, if Pentecostalism had been stillborn, if Catholic canonizations had slowed to a crawl in the twentieth and twenty-first centuries, then atheists would be crowing, comparing the supposed saintly intercessions of the Catholic past to the counterfeit relics that circulated in the Middle Ages, and generally claiming vindication for disenchanted theories of the world.

Yet no less than the experience of mystical encounters, the experience of miracles persists, with the same potential implications as in premodernity: that there are more things in heaven and earth than can be measured and distilled by scientific materialism, a Shakespearean wisdom that stands undefeated by four subsequent centuries of supposed disenchantment.

## Romancing the Numinous

So what do skeptics, our latter-day Humeans and Horatios, say to this persistence? Several things, to which I'll try to do some justice here.

First, they complain that while mystical and miraculous-seeming incidents may get written up as case studies by doctors or researchers, they still fail all the formal tests of modern science, insofar as they resist laboratory study, they rely on individual accounts, and they cannot be replicated under double-blind control-trial conditions. This is effectively a variation on Hume's original critique of belief in the supernatural—that by definition extraordinary claims should require extraordinary evidence to compel belief, and the claims of mystical happenings do not even meet the prosaic bar that we use to determine, say, whether to prescribe a cancer drug or approve a cough medicine for sales in pharmacies.

The difficulty with this argument is that it presumes that the supernatural is effectively the equivalent of an incredibly low-probability material event, which if it were real should happen consistently, indeed automatically, under some set of highly unusual but ultimately replicable conditions. But the religious worldview assumes that these happenings are, at least in the more dramatic cases, the results of the free decisions of nonhuman persons with whom we can interact through prayer or magic—God Himself, the gods, angelic or demonic beings, the holy dead, unclassifiable forces.

The most common kinds of mystical experience, the ones that

just involve the self's experience of its relationship to the cosmos or to its own mortal flesh, *can* be reproduced to some degree under laboratory conditions. You can put the meditating monk in the MRI machine, you can get general replications of experiences (the details are another matter) among people going on an ayahuasca-mediated spiritual trip. But the encounter with something entirely other, in which the other being or force or personality has agency as well, is just not the kind of thing that the scientific method is designed to measure or test, nor is it the kind of event to which it makes sense to assign definite probabilities.

Consider, by way of analogy, the sexual and romantic relationships between men and women. There are aspects of attraction that are amenable to laboratory investigation: you can show people photos of members of the opposite sex and get generalizable and predictable patterns about what they report as alluring or off-putting, and you can hook people up to various pieces of equipment, show them stimulating photos or videos, and generate fairly predictable reactions in terms of blood flow and arousal.

But as you move from general patterns of attraction to the specifics of a particular male-female pairing, from generic lust to actual romance, predictability and replicability diminishes and finally disappears. The algorithm of a well-designed dating site can give you (well, maybe) a range of women or men with whom you're more likely to click, but the clicking itself is far too bound up in the agency of actual individuals to be predicted in advance. Friends and matchmakers and sociological data can all push you in a promising direction, but no scientist can tell you whether you will fall in love, or when, or whether the other person will love you back. And it is neither a failure of science nor proof of the nonexistence of romantic infatuation that this kind of prediction is inherently impossible; it just reflects the challenge of incorporating individual agency and personality into the mechanisms of scientific assessment.

From the religious perspective, something similar is going on with the mystical and supernatural landscapes. Just as you're less likely to experience love or even infatuation if you make no effort whatsoever to connect with the opposite sex (and, indeed, you may find yourself doubting that the true love described by romantics even exists), you are less likely to have a mystical experience if you never go in search of one—although you still never know when you might be smacked upside the head. Becoming a religious seeker raises your odds of some kind of mystical experience or communion, just as making various love-oriented choices—going to singles' events, hanging out in mixed-sex spaces, joining a dating app—makes it more likely that some form of romance will ensue. But there are gradations to this experience: just as it's seemingly easier to experience the more generic kinds of mystical feeling than something more dramatic and personal and weird, it's easier to experience lust than infatuation, easier to experience infatuation than real love, and at each level the predictability diminishes.

In the end, the fact that you are dealing with another person's agency, the specific feelings and choices of the potential beloved, yields an inherent individuality to the experience that defies prediction and replicability entirely. As does your own individuality, the difference between meeting a potential lover when you're in one mood versus another, the influence of all kinds of contingent forces on the state of your self on any given date—and then the mutual interaction between what's going on with you and what's going on with the other person in the course of your initial interactions and your courtship. There is a reason that love is talked about so often in terms of serendipity: you can predict where it might befall you, but beyond those general conditions you are as much in the hands of Aphrodite as any religious seeker hoping for a brush with God.

There are various limits to this analogy. For one thing more people think they've experienced true love than have experienced the numinous. About two-thirds of Americans claim to know what true love feels like, compared with about half who claim some kind of mystical encounter.[22] For another, while true love is too idiosyncratic and personal to be predicted, the physical existence of the beloved can be empirically demonstrated: you can put your girlfriend in a laboratory setting (if you ask nicely, at least) even if you can't predict what will make her marry you, whereas the Being and beings encountered mystically are obviously invisible in the everyday.

But if there were incorporeal beings with whom human beings could commune, if all the claims of the world's religions and all the attestations of their mystics corresponded to some supernatural reality, there would be nothing remotely surprising in the fact that the strongest forms of communion couldn't be predicted in advance or re-created in a laboratory. The unpredictability is built into the hypothesis. The miracle or the vision or the demonic reaching-in is supposed to be specific to the individual; your own internal condition plays some unmeasurable role; and likewise the external agents can't be subjected to normal scientific forms of scrutiny because they're agents and not just impersonal forces—and their own purposes and interests, for our good or ill, involve not being subjected to the rules that govern our material existence.

There are things you can do that make them more likely to appear. If you want to meet a demon, practice Satanism. (Please don't.) If you want to find case studies of miraculous healing, go looking among people who pray intensely for such things. And I don't want to insist on the absolute impossibility of doing empirical studies in these areas, since to some degree a presumptive disbelief in the supernatural leads Official Knowledge to dismiss interesting work on topics like ESP or healing prayer even when it's being conducted with impressive rigor.[23]

But still, the spirits get a veto over your effort to summon them, and "you shall not put the Lord your God to the test."[24] If He exists, you're in His laboratory, and He decides when to suspend its rules.

## Is It All inside Your Head?

Fair enough, the skeptic might reply, but why not take this insight in a different direction? If spiritual experience is commonplace but inherently personal, if the individual aspect makes it poorly suited for laboratory replication, why shouldn't we still explain it in terms of the idiosyncratic psychology of the person experiencing it, rather than assuming that other minds are involved as well? Dreams, for instance, are personal, subjective, intimate; you can predict when a person will dream but not what they will dream about. But dreams are still understood to be products of the individual's mind, associated with specific brain states and generated by certain mysterious subconscious processes; even people who believe in mystical or prophetic dreams do not generally believe that all dreams involve tuning in to an externally sourced broadcast.

Likewise certain forms of mental illness generate unusual experiences—hearing voices, seeing visions—that our ancestors treated as divine encounters but we now treat as medical conditions. So why shouldn't other mystical encounters in waking life under sane conditions be regarded as part of the same continuum? Those dreams that happen without the mediation of sleep, "hallucinations of the sane" that are temporary rather than chronic, illusions that come over us for poorly understood reasons but are ultimately grounded exclusively in the activity within our brains?

Buttressing this theory is our ability to study mystical experience in its basic form—to see that, for instance, the experience of oneness with the universe experienced in meditation correlates with diminishing activity in the portion of the brain that seems to regulate boundaries. If the brain is somehow involved in such feelings, why not just assume that the brain generates them? Likewise, the fact that certain spiritual experiences are associated with the ingestion of herbs and pharmaceuticals and hallucinogens tells us that some material substrate is involved in those sorts of encounters—so why not assume that the brain is generating the encounter spontaneously in cases where LSD and shrooms and ayahuasca aren't involved?

One response starts with a point made in the last chapter: the fact that our consciousness encounters reality through the mediation of the flesh doesn't mean that the experience of consciousness can be easily reduced to chemical reactions in the body and brain. Similarly, the fact that spiritual experiences have neurological correlates, and indeed that manipulating your brain and body can make spiritual experiences more likely or more intense, doesn't make the experiences themselves inherently hallucinogenic or unreal.

The world's religious traditions have always assumed that normal everyday enfleshed reality needs to be reset a bit, shaken up or tested or reshaped, to make it easier for the embedded consciousness to encounter more ethereal realities. After all, if normal biological functioning yielded easily to the supernatural we would have supernatural experiences all the time!

That's why fasting, mortification, vision quests, and yes, plants and drugs and other substances have all found places in spiritual disciplines worldwide. No ancient hermit, wrestling with devils in the desert, would be surprised that his body exhibited changes before and during the experience. Pushing his flesh toward spiritual openness is why he went into the desert in the first place. Freeman Dyson, the brilliant and eccentric physicist, made the same point about attempts to research paranormal phenomena. Again and again, he wrote in the *New York Review of Books*, the most credible and dramatic examples occur "only when people are under stress and experiencing strong emotion."[25] But it doesn't explain away an apparently psychic experience to say that it's linked to dramatic changes in the experiencer's brain chemistry; the would-be reductionist still has to explain the specifics of the experience itself.

Nor from a Darwinian perspective does the presence of some sort of spiritual-experience functionality within the brain tell us that the functions themselves are false creations. Most evolutionary theorizing goes back and forth between portraying spiritual experience as some sort of beneficial illusion and treating it as a "spandrel," an accidental byproduct of other features selected for by competitive pressures. But both theories presume materialism and atheism. Presume otherwise, and if generally sane and healthy people experience consistent reactions in their brains that correlate with what they describe as experiences of transcendence, joy, divine unity, or personal revelation, a strict evolutionary account could just as easily suggest that like other features of our mammalian brain, any "spiritual-experience module" or set of "God neurons" evolved to match something important in reality itself.

Then the specific nature of intense spiritual experiences and their neurological correlates raise further questions about a strictly materialist account. We know what dreams are like—confused, bizarre, illogical or dream-logical, fraught with symbolism but lacking in coherence, hard to remember unless you quickly write them down, their fundamental unreality quickly recognized upon waking. Some spiritual "trips" can have a similar quality, but the higher-level experiences have the opposite quality: they are often described as more real than reality itself, far more memorable than ordinary existence, the usual order of things giving way to something deeper and much more vivid and profound.

This is true of encounters like Barbara Ehrenreich's or my mother's—a feeling of hyperreality that endures after the godlike spirit has departed. It's especially true of near-death experiences, the encounters with loved ones and angels and heavenly intimations (and, again, sometimes hellish ones) that people experience when their bodies are failing, from which they tend to return transformed—with vivid recollections, a radically different metaphysical perspective, and personal peace coexisting with a sense of moral awakening.[26] And it's also true, interestingly, of certain mystical experiences associated with DMT, the active chemical ingredient in ayahuasca, the kind of psychedelic most likely to induce not just a generic mystical feeling but specific encounters with supernatural-seeming beings. (Notably, users often report seeing the same kinds of beings—angelic, demonic, extraterrestrial or elven-seeming—even when they're unaware of other people's trips.)[27]

What's notable about this hyperreality is that it's not connected to hyperactivity in the brain itself. To the contrary: like other hallucinogens but more so, DMT seems to shut down or reduce various forms of brain functioning. Meanwhile the brain on the threshold of death is even more diminished in its capabilities, seemingly primed for fundamentally chaotic and hallucinatory experiences—but the closer to death the personal experience, in many cases, the greater its clarity and intensity and sense of underlying order. A recent study of near-death experiences in the European journal *Resuscitation* noted what it called the "paradoxical finding of lucidity and heightened reality when brain function is severely disordered, or has ceased"—with the paradox, the authors mildly suggested, being a reason for scientists to "consider alternatives" to the belief that consciousness is simply an "epiphenomenon" of the brain itself.[28]

One alternative to that materialist belief, favored by theorists of psychedelics all the way back to Aldous Huxley but hardly limited to them, is the idea that the brain is a kind of valve or reducing agent, which limits the potential experiences and encounters available to our consciousness in order to enable us to live normally within material reality. If this were the case, you would expect that diminishing the brain's activity through prayer or meditation, changing its internal calibration, or going through a partial shutdown process (e.g. death) would be, in fact, the kind of mind-opening experience that's reported by mystics, psychedelic users, and people who seemingly cross the border between life and death. Lucidity and intensity and cosmic wonder can all increase, in other words, as the brain's reducing function weakens—not because the brain is misfiring or hallucinating but because the mind or soul is being partially released from its mooring to material reality.

# Imagine There's No Mystical Experience

To the hardened materialist all of this sounds fantastic. But consider the kinds of explanations for a phenomenon like near-death experiences that materialism requires you to accept. Under its premises the human brain somehow evolved a capacity to generate some of its most intense and memorable experiences, hallucinations far more powerful, coherent, and seemingly realistic than those available to dreamers in the pink of physical health, in the incredibly narrow window between the brain going into irreversible crisis and life being fully extinguished. (I am granting for the sake of argument the materialist premise that some brain activity persists during near-death experiences, though there are cases in which this seems doubtful.)

This capacity either evolved accidentally, the dying brain taking flashes of light and out-of-body sensations and other effects randomly generated by its spasms and weaving them into a tapestry richer than any normal dream, more consistent across cultures than any hallucination—like a cathedral being created as a byproduct of a mudslide. Or else it conferred some notable evolutionary advantage, notwithstanding the fact that the overwhelming majority of people having these experiences would then proceed to actually expire, making them entirely irrelevant to both the future life of the person herself and to the early hominid culture to which her narrative might otherwise have provided some sort of religious comfort. That potential comfort, in fact, only became widely available under twentieth-century conditions, when our medical technologies finally began reviving enough people to make it clear that this was a commonplace phenomenon.

Humans, being endlessly inventive, have made many engaging attempts to vindicate the adaptiveness of near-death experiences against this kind of raised eyebrow. For instance, I have a paper in front of me right now that tries to explain them as an elaborate expansion of thanatosis, the "playing dead" tactic that prey animals use as a last-ditch defense against predators—the idea being that a feigned death is likely to be more convincing if your mind actually believes that it's headed to the afterlife.[29]

This isn't a completely terrible explanation for the near-death experiences associated with the mere expectation of dying—for instance, those people who survive falls from great heights sometimes report a version of the "life review" phenomenon, a kind of rapid shuttling-through of memories, often woven together with a sense of retrospective moral judgment, just before they land. How it would explain the richly detailed heavenly experiences of totally unconscious patients suffering cardiac arrest on the operating table is less clear. (Moreover, in the paper's most compelling anecdote, a riveting account of a near-death experience that took place while a teenage girl was about to be devoured by a tiger, the near-death experience comes across as extremely evolutionarily nonadvantageous, leaving the girl at the predator's mercy until some part of her mind screamed, "You're only fifteen!" and wrenched her soul out of the heavenly landscape and back into survival mode.)

But if your premises require some kind of evolutionary just-so story to explain anything that hints at supernatural possibilities, you can probably find one that leaves those premises safely undisturbed. While you hunt for one, though, I would ask you to imagine a world where these kinds of experiences didn't happen—where nobody came back from the threshold of death with a life-changing account of light suffused with love, where the experiences of the dying in at least 99.9 percent of cases were just a random dreamlike jumble, and where as science advanced in resuscitative powers, it became clear that whatever garbled legends about near-death experiences were handed down from ancient Egypt or medieval Europe, nobody whose heart stopped on a modern operating table encountered anything except a dying cerebellum's madhouse followed by the void.

In such a world, that void would seem like a reasonably telling point against many forms of religion. The believers could prattle on all they liked about heaven or hell, afterlives or reincarnation or divine judgments, angels and ancestral shades. But the scientists and doctors would be able to say, definitively, that when they pulled people back from the doorway, all that came back with them were ravings or the nonreports that you'd expect from entering the Big Nothing.

But then turnabout is only fair. In this world, this reality, where stranger and richer experiences conspicuously do happen on death's door, and where scientific modernity has revealed more of this richness and strangeness and cross-cultural consistency than we ever knew before—including, for God's sake, the fact that many dying people really have all their memories brought back to them and replayed under a frame of moral judgment—you have to acknowledge that faith has won a provisional point from atheism, that on this front the reasons to take religion seriously have multiplied rather than diminished.

## Michael Shermer's Residue

Finally, a purely psychological explanation for religious experience, one that seeks to encompass all of mysticism in the workings and delusions of the mind, still falls short when it comes to explaining away the moments when the mystical seems to affect material reality. Neurological illusions don't explain Shermer's awakened radio, or Lurhmann's smoking battery, or why a nun's incurable Parkinson's disease disappeared instantly the night she asked for the late Pope John Paul II's intervention (to pick the reported miracle that sealed his sainthood). The skeptics need a narrative that disenchants these kinds of happenings as well—one that goes beyond the persistence of fakery and fraud and misremembering, which certainly explains a number of miraculous-seeming happenings but leaves a core of impossibilities untouched.

In skeptical argument, some of these remaining cases are pinned on coincidence and the law of large numbers, where given world and time enough there will be correlations between extremely unlikely happenings and people praying for those happenings to come along. Thus a patient delivered from a seemingly incurable condition might just be a vanishingly rare example of spontaneous remission intersecting with the happenstance of a prayer being offered at a particularly timely moment—two slim probabilities converging in a way that, in a big world where lots of things are happening, slim probabilities sometimes do. The batteries starting a fire in an academic's bag while she felt spiritual power course through her might be an example of spontaneous combustion happening to coincide with a self-generated sense of mystical experience coinciding with spiritual reading; accidental fires do happen, this one just seemed supernatural because of the happenstance of timing.

These law-of-large-numbers explanations are satisfying in certain cases. If I had a dream twenty years ago that seemed to eerily anticipate some future event, well, we have a lot of dreams; the odds are good that a few of them across a life cycle will seem accidentally prophetic. Such explanations, though, inevitably seem more unsatisfying the more extreme the happenstance. If we have zero examples of a medical condition going into complete and immediate remission, and the only example involves intercessory prayer, it's hard not to consider the prayer as a relevant variable rather than an accident.

But the absence of satisfying explanations, the skeptics argue, is also something we should expect, because all human theories of the cosmos are necessarily incomplete, and any attempt at general explanation will leave what Shermer calls the "residue problem"—in which "no matter how comprehensive a theory is, there will always be a residue of anomalies for which it cannot account."[30]

But as Shermer himself notes, as human knowledge progresses we usually expect further theorizing to resolve part of the residue—as, say, Einstein's theory of relativity resolved issues left unexplained by Newton's gravitational theory. And at some point, the fact that such a large residue of the unexplained clusters around religious experience and spiritual questing, the fact that within that larger cluster there are subclusters that seem to fit with all the old specific ideas of religion—the accessibility of both an impersonal spiritual landscape and personal gods, the availability of divine guides and demonic enemies and ambiguous spirits, the possibility of an afterlife, the power of prayer—should suggest the parsimonious conclusion that the theory that best explains this particular residue is, in fact, the religious worldview that most human beings in most ages have taken more or less for granted.

Especially since the alternatives to this possibility have the same difficulties as the nonreligious theories of the cosmos and our consciousness that we considered in prior chapters. For instance, both the complexity, resilience, and seeming realism of so much supernatural experience and the apparent miracles associated with religious interventions are sometimes explained atheistically by hyping up the extraordinary powers of the human mind. Our own subconsciousness, in this telling, generates everything from perceived alien abductions to perceived near-death experiences out of some deep storehouse of Jungian archetypes, some vast undiscovered country that we only access normally in dreams or maybe through taking psychedelics. And these regions of the mind have powers over the body that we can't fully fathom, of which the placebo effect offers just the barest hint—such that in certain cases a strong religious belief alone, triggered to special intensity by prayer or crisis, is somehow enough to make sickened flesh heal itself, to defeat a disease or roll back a spreading cancer.

The problem is that at a certain point this kind of "high" view of consciousness seems indistinguishable from supernaturalism, concentrating godlike powers in a psyche that does not plausibly reduce back to neurons and brain chemistry any more than does the mysterious experience of the conscious mind. Where is this psyche, exactly? Where in your brain tissue lives this rich and fertile subconscious?

How exactly does its apparently immense but entirely invisible creativity emerge from a purely physical substrate and then transform that substrate when some kind of healing power is required? How is attributing supernatural-seeming happenings to such a mysterious, invisible emanation of physical embodiment distinct from attributing them to a spirit or a soul, an angel or a god?

Then there is the alternative that Shermer comes around to in his own determinedly atheistic attempt to wrestle with the seemingly supernatural intervention at his wedding, the grit in his materialist's shoe. Citing the movie *Interstellar*, in which an apparent poltergeist turns out to be Matthew McConaughey's character reaching back through an interdimensional portal to his daughter, he imagines his wife's grandfather somehow occupying a similar "multidimensional tesseract in which he can see her at all times of her life simultaneously," and using "gravitational waves near a black hole or a wormhole to turn on his old radio for his granddaughter."

Such a scenario, he posits, "would be fully explicable by physical laws and forces as we understand them."[31] Well, phew.

"The materialist," G. K. Chesterton wrote a century ago, "is not allowed to admit into his spotless machine the slightest speck of spiritualism or miracle." He may not "retain even the tiniest imp, though it might be hiding in a pimpernel."[32]

Back then materialists were a bit more confident that all the imps, large and small, could be eventually reduced away, or dissolved like dew in the bright rays of science. It is to their credit, to Shermer's credit, that he now acknowledges otherwise, conceding that there will always be a residue, that there's no way to fully scrub away the remnants of fairyland, the rumor of angels, the hints of hell and heaven.

But he has made his decision about what this residue must mean. We have already seen that it seems better to skeptics to posit an infinity of invisible universes, all inaccessible to one another, rather than make a concession to the seeming evidence for intelligence and order and design. Apparently it is also better to insist that a near-infinity of times and places are being contemplated and bridged through some itself-impossible-seeming interdimensional technique mastered by some genius elsewhere in the multiverse, every time a very little miracle happens to an unsuspecting atheist, than for that atheist to consider the possibility that God might be giving him a wink.

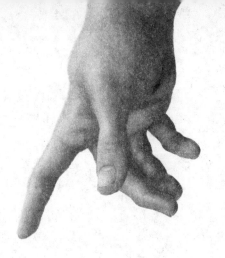

4

# The Case for
# Commitment

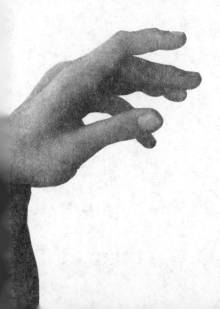

Late, very late, at a Christmas party in mid-2000s Washington, DC, I found myself trapped in a small kitchen with Christopher Hitchens, the scourge of faith who loved to argue with the pious, so much so that they often assumed that he was just one brilliant thrust or successful parry away from throwing in with God.

On this occasion I was much too tired or too intoxicated to do my part for the cause of Hitchens' soul. But my attempts at extrication were unsuccessful, because Hitchens was building to a question he clearly considered urgent, if not devastating.

"Suppose," he said to me, index finger extended, an upright platter rising like a halo from the shelf behind his head—"Suppose that Jesus of Nazareth really did rise from the dead."

"Okay," I said, "let's suppose He did."

"Well, then what exactly would that really *prove*?"

I don't remember how I responded in the moment; the question was more memorably unexpected than any possible riposte. But I thought of Hitchens' words many years later while pilfering some of the neuroscientist Erik Hoel's arguments for the second chapter of this book. After elaborating all the limits of contemporary neuroscience, all the ways in which it fails to offer a basic theory of the thing it's trying to investigate, Hoel acknowledges the possibility that the religious critics of materialism have a point, and that a satisfactory theory of mind will never be extracted from "the extrinsic machinations of the world." In which case, he writes, there will always be a "slight crack in the door that refuses to close all the way," a slight hope that maybe the death of the physical brain isn't the end of consciousness—a hope, in other words, in the possibility that life continues after death.

And yet, he goes on, what can that kind of "incompleteness" in science's materialist ambitions possibly demonstrate about the cosmos or our place in it? Nothing: The slight crack in the door is just a thin line of light, and the shadows are too deep: "Scientific incompleteness would recommend no particular religion, no specific revelation other than uncertainty. It would mean that this world is like a great ancient aurochs, its breath steaming in the cold, its eyes a mirror of dark glass, its face bovine and unreadable. Decipher the expression if you will."[1]

As with Hitchens in the pantry, the concession that there might actually be mind behind matter, even life awaiting beyond death, yields a conclusion of futility: what would that really prove?

A third example of the mentality I'm describing: In the final season of *The Sopranos*, a season that begins with Tony Soprano having an extended near-death experience, Paulie Gualtiere, one of Tony's capos and the show's most superstitious character, confesses to his boss that he once had a vision of the Virgin Mary in the Jersey mob's strip club, the Bada Bing. Tony doesn't tell Paulie that it was just a hallucination or that the Queen of Heaven wasn't really there; he just stresses—mobster to mobster, murderer to murderer—that Paulie shouldn't let it get in the way of his everyday obligations.

"I'm not saying there's nothing out there," he says. "But you gotta live your life."

In their different ways Hitchens, Hoel, and Tony are all expressing a commonplace response to the arguments I've marshaled in this book so far: not so much a defiance of religious possibilities as a kind of helplessness in the face of the universe's mystery, and a default to simply doing nothing in response.

In this spirit, one can imagine a reader conceding a great deal to my sketch of the human situation—acknowledging the appearances of order and design, the deep mystery of consciousness, the peculiarly privileged-seeming position of human beings in the cosmos, the resilience of mystical experiences and seemingly supernatural happenings—and still circling back around to Hitchens' so-what-does-it-prove, to Hoel's vision of the cosmos as an inscrutable mystery beast, to Tony telling his friend not to lose sleep over the unknowable.

This is why I'm trying to emphasize the convergence of different forms of evidence, not a single line of argument alone. For my own part I think that the default to helplessness is mistaken no matter what. Just taken individually, the possibility that someone might rise from the grave, or that our minds might survive our bodily deaths, or that the Something Out There might yield supernatural visions even to a New Jersey mobster, should each demand a serious response from any rational creature. If Jesus possibly rose from the dead, you don't need to automatically become a Christian (maybe the Christians interpreted it all wrong), but as a mortal being yourself you should probably be interested in His story. If the door to immortality— real immortality, not the Silicon Valley aspiration to somehow undo cellular aging or merge our minds with AI—is possibly cracked open, you should probably think about making some kind of preparation for whatever might be waiting on the other side. If a vision of transcendent goodness and mercy appears to you, a sinner, and you don't understand what it means, the most obvious interpretation is that you gotta change your life.

But you don't have to agree with me, because the world doesn't ask you to make a leap toward faith or belief based on just a single prompting—one potential resurrection, one apparent limit on scientific certainty, one strip-club supernatural vision. Rather it offers multiple prompts, multiple indicators, converging and overlapping and all pointing the human intellect in a similar direction—with strong indications of cosmic order and design *and* a strong possibility of human significance within that order *and* good reasons to think that we can reach up toward the supernatural even as the supernatural reaches out or down to us.

The point is that there's an array of flashing lights, not just a one-off illumination inside the shadows of the Bada Bing. If mind might well precede matter, *and* the laws of the universe indicate that some intelligence created and sustains existence, *and* human reason seems to have a privileged ability to unlock existence's mysterious underlying order, *and* the seemingly supernatural intrudes upon the natural as often in the modern world as in the past—well, then, you, as a man or a woman trying to chart the best course through a finite lifespan, with difficult moral choices at every turn and death awaiting sooner rather than later, have every reason to take a pretty strong interest in the story you've found yourself inside, what part you might be asked to play in it, and how, for you and everyone, it might ultimately end.

And as it happens there exists in our world civilization, as in every prior human civilization worthy of the name, a vast body of personal writing and reporting and theorizing and argument on exactly these pretty-damn-important matters. There exists a substantial set of practices and rituals and wisdom literatures that is supposed to align human consciousness with cosmic purpose, that claim to help unite the individual human story with the larger drama, and to make sure that your soul is both prepared for that potentially cracked door at the conclusion of your life and protected from forces that might not want you to successfully pass through.

All of this religion offers—right now, today, as you read these words. Once you concede that the universe might be a bit more than just a collision of atoms doing meaningless expansions and contractions, you are not standing alone next to an enigmatic aurochs, staring with bafflement into its inhuman eyes. No, you are standing in the same place that generations of human beings have found themselves before: at the beginning of a journey, a quest, a pilgrim's progress, that you have good reason to believe is going somewhere quite important, somewhere of ultimate significance. And the choice this book is concerned with, the choice to become religious or not, is fundamentally a choice between looking around at the piled-up knapsacks and guidebooks that prior pilgrims have carried and used and written, and deciding to see what they might have to offer—or just wandering onward, willfully blind without a compass or a map.

# The Maps and the Territory

*But there are so many different maps*, comes the response. Yes, indeed: most of the claims I've been making about reality and the human situation are general; religions are inevitably and fatefully specific. Acknowledging the apparent ordering of the universe doesn't tell us what kind of divine intelligence might have ordered it, or resolve any of the questions that have divided religious faiths since time immemorial. Acknowledging the compelling nature of spiritual experience doesn't vindicate any particular religious system; most such experiences are too individual and personal and culturally mediated for that. Recognizing the cosmic privilege of human consciousness doesn't yield certainty about what we're called to do with that privilege—what kind of morality we're obliged to follow, what aspirations we should embrace, which prayers and which rituals best fulfill our nature and connect to our purpose in the world.

My argument in the preceding chapters, and throughout this book, is that the basic justifications for a religious worldview are readily accessible to a reasonable human being—that the universe isn't really hiding the ball from us when it comes to cosmic order and human exceptionalism and even supernatural happenings, and that modern nonbelief often amounts to an attempt to hide the ball from ourselves. But the likelihood of a specific faith tradition being capital-T True is not nearly as readily accessible. So if the refusal to do anything at all after acknowledging religious possibilities is unreasonable, stubborn, even senseless, a reluctance to narrow oneself to a particular religious tradition—to pick up just one backpack, just one map—is more rational and defensible.

Especially since one thing that separates readers of this book from the typical human being in the more religious past is the simple availability of multiple traditions, the breadth of spiritual options that liberalism and pluralism and globalization have opened up. All the old reasons for being religious may still obtain today, but the circumstances for the person interested in religion are quite different. If you were born in thirteenth-century France or eighteenth-century Arabia you pretty much had to embrace the set of traditions handed down to you, risking ostracism or persecution if you were too innovative or experimental. But now the range of options is far wider, and so are the possibilities for personalization, for remixing, for taking from multiple traditions, for trying to make your own discoveries, pack your own knapsack, and discover your own map.

As a starting place for someone with no definite ideas about religion beyond the sudden realization of its importance, there is nothing wrong with this approach. Just as you wouldn't expect someone newly introduced to the concept of politics to immediately become an ideological activist, or someone unexpectedly dropped into a novel PhD program to become immediately bound to a single interpretative school, becoming newly interested in religion should be at first a mind-opening experience, a chance to explore without prejudice, to take ideas seriously without the temptations of team spirit. And not only ideas but experiences—different forms of communion, worship, prayer.

But this beginning is not where you should hope to end. In a finite lifespan, replete with urgent moral choices and destined to end with a voyage to the undiscovered country, permanent open-mindedness is not necessarily a virtue. In the end the meaningful life is usually the committed life; the dilettante's posture must yield at some point to the active choice. Better to face the consequences of even a mistaken commitment or decision than to hear, at the last, the fateful judgment, "because you are lukewarm, and neither hot nor cold, I will spit you out of my mouth."[2]

## Not Everyone Can Be a Prophet

*Spit you out*—that's a harsh judgment, surely! And also perhaps unfair to the religious individualist, the sincere but solitary pilgrim.

What if someone were not lukewarm but passionate and committed to beliefs that belong to them and them alone? Would they too stand condemned for simply being true to their own explorations, loyal to the truth that their journey discovered? Especially given the evidence, discussed in the last chapter, for the universality of certain kinds of religious experience across different societies and cultures, why shouldn't we take for granted the existence of multiple paths to God, and set out to forge one on our own? Why is trying to be the master of your own religious fate, the captain of your soul, somehow inferior to showing up at a particular building on a particular day of the week, embracing a packaged set of dogmas or beliefs, and binding oneself to all the sins and fallibilities attached to all the world's significant religions?

There are several answers to these reasonable questions. The first is the simplest: you are probably not a religious genius.

I said "probably"! Maybe you are especially favored by divine revelation or graced with a once-in-a-generation theological acuity—in which the case for commitment is admittedly a bit weaker than for the rest of us ordinary mortals. But the idea that you are better off putting together a religious worldview entirely on your own, simply taking a bit here from one faith or a bit there from another, presumes a lot upon the strength of your individual intellect and moral compass, to say nothing of more supernatural questions. It may be theoretically possible to generate a healthy way of being religious in this way. But unless you have a very high opinion of yourself, or of God's special favor, it's not the natural way to bet.

This holds true across multiple different ways of thinking about the major religious traditions. You can think of each religion primarily as a corpus of ideas, a set of interlocking beliefs and theories established across many centuries of reflection and debate, honed for plausibility and internal coherence in the same way as more secular systems of thought that have survived the centuries. This process by no means guarantees correctness, but it establishes a conversation that a new practitioner can usefully join while assuming the stability of some parameters, the reasonability of certain assumptions, the basic consistency of the world-picture allowing for certain knots and tensions. And for most people this will have obvious advantages over setting yourself up as the founder of the school of one.

Or you can think of a faith tradition as a technology for bringing the soul into alignment with cosmic powers, an evolved web of prayer and ritual and mystical tradition in which the intellectual commitments are less important than the practice. Here again, the better part of wisdom lies in assuming that the web evolved this way for a reason, that there's wisdom to be found in the crowd and the multigenerational (or multimillennial) inheritance that exceeds the individual's capacities alone. Certainly this is true of every secular practice worth pursuing, from sports to poker to watercolor painting. The rules and traditions aren't arbitrary; the ways to practice and improve are handed down for necessary reasons. A plan where you bring soccer tactics into field hockey can probably wait until you've apprenticed deeply in the sport. And the fact that the stakes are higher in committing to a religious tradition than in choosing a favorite game or art form or hobby only confirms the wisdom of trying to join in humbly at some point, rather than imagining that the goal is to invent something entirely personalized, entirely new.

This is even true, crucially, if you take the optimistic view that all the religious maps, or at least most of them, lead to the same destination in the end. Lots of people who are moderately favorable to religion but disinclined to pick one faith and stick with it offer this justification for their dilettantism, but it doesn't really hold up to scrutiny. Suppose you were in Bangor in 1887 and you wanted to reach Topeka and you were told that there were five excellent maps, from very different mapmakers, offering very different itineraries, that would all eventually lead you from Maine west to Kansas. Would it make sense to say, *Well, since they all get you there eventually, I'm sure I can just draw my own map and get the same result*? Would it make sense to stitch pieces of them together, rejecting the boring or grinding parts of each route, on the theory that this way your journey would be nothing but fun visits to neat roadside attractions? Of course not. If you want to reach Topeka, the fact that you respect all the different mapmakers equally doesn't absolve you of the requirement to choose one, to follow, to submit.

This submission also doesn't require total certainty about the tradition that you're joining. Some religions explicitly allow for all kinds of uncertainty, and just as modernity has multiplied religious options it has also multiplied religious institutions that try to accommodate the uncertain pilgrim. This accommodation might be more extensive in a tradition like Hinduism, with its extreme multiplicity of schools, than in the more dogmatic traditions of the West. But the liberal religious programs in Christianity and Judaism exist, in part, to offer the benefits of Western monotheism to people who aren't sure about all its doctrinal claims or communal requirements, to offer general maps to questers who aren't sure about the entire guidebook.

The more conservative confessions ask more of their practitioners; my own Catholic Church expects converts to profess fidelity to *all* the church believes and teaches. But in practice they too are filled with people who maintain private heresies or private doubts, who feel agnostic two days out of seven—but who have made the sensible decision that it's better to live inside the tradition they consider most plausible while holding doubts than to reject any system in the name of those difficulties.

Meanwhile, the same pluralism that multiplies your religious choices also means that you aren't trapped with them. If you live inside a specific system for a decade and lose faith in it entirely, you are allowed to change your mind and leave, to drop its map and choose another. Commitment comes with risks and costs, but it isn't a one-way ticket, and nobody in the Western religious mainstream is currently asking you to join a church you absolutely can't escape. The perfectly open-minded attitude should yield at some point to commitment, but the committed mind doesn't have to become entirely closed. You can reap the benefits of walking humbly with a tradition without feeling like you're sealing yourself inside a cult.

## No Believer Is an Island

Those benefits include the second reason for choosing commitment over splendid isolation: human beings need community, and most things worth doing are worth doing with other people's support. Again, this is obvious in secular affairs. One might reasonably set out to learn about politics initially through individual reading and research, but it would be extremely peculiar to claim to "do politics" without finally joining some kind of collective enterprise. Likewise with other passions and pursuits: from sports teams to hobbyist clubs to twelve-step groups, it isn't just that being in community with other human beings carries the generic relational benefits of friendships and support networks and simple human contact. It's that the pursuit itself is almost always more fully embraced and practiced and lived out through communal contacts, interpersonal relationships, shared activities. You can't really play soccer alone, and if you do you won't get very good at it. There's no reason to think that making contact with your moral purpose and supernatural destiny would be any different.

Not that the social benefits of joining a religion should be dismissed; they are substantial, meaningful, and the best sociological case for practicing a faith independent of whether you believe in it, and for preferring a society with strong religious institutions to one where every man or woman is a church unto themselves.

But in this book we're concerned with religion for its own sake, with eternal stakes and not just sociological ones. So the key argument for being part of a religious community—to whatever extent, in a fulsome form if possible but an attenuated form if that's all you can manage at the start—is that it makes you more likely to actively practice your religion, to take its dictates and admonitions seriously, to seek the will of Providence regularly rather than intermittently, to live out the moral vision that the faith holds up.

This can happen through the same interpersonal mechanisms that deliver religion's social benefits: you join a religion and make friends who also practice that religion, over time your social network reinforces your religious habits in both direct ways (a weekly Bible study) and indirect ways (a desire to see your friends at synagogue), you are more likely to meet a spouse who shares your faith and encourages its practice, and so on.

But even without strong friendships and relationships, or even before they begin to form, just the example of other people performing the same rites and rituals around you, week in and week out, can deepen your own commitment, your sense of the sacred, your impetus to further conversion. And if you insist, with a version of the Tony Soprano shrug, that you've tried religion, you've read some books and said some prayers and received nothing revelatory in return, then you're in the position of someone interested in soccer who refuses to join a team and play consistently. I won't disbelieve in your sincerity, but I will sincerely doubt your effort.

Prior even to the effects of seeing other people practicing a religion, there is the potential effect of just setting foot regularly inside the building or space where they practice. "A serious house on serious earth it is, / In whose blent air all our compulsions meet, / Are recognised, and robed as destinies."[3] That's the unhappily unbelieving Philip Larkin's description of church and churchgoing, which captures as well as any believer's writing the special place of sacred architecture in grounding spiritual communities, in preparing the people who enter for their religious obligations, in creating a link between the horizontal and the vertical, the gathered believers and supernatural possibilities. Before any kind of joining and professing or cobelieving, just entering and praying consistently in such a space is already a step out of solipsism and into communion with the living and dead.

Of course there is nothing foolproof here. Not every beautiful form of sacred architecture nurtures a resilient religious community, and not every successful-seeming religious community is actually a spiritually healthy place to end up. Certainly in a society where professed faith is a default and almost everyone is participating in a religious tradition, there is a grave temptation toward hypocrisy, fake piety, the kinds of empty spiritual practice that the world's great religions warn against almost as often as they warn against active impiety or unbelief. And there are certainly communities in our own society where this socially conditioned pretense of religion still exists.

But in most regions of contemporary culture, and certainly for most people hesitating on the threshold of religion, the dangers of hypocrisy and fake piety are relatively distant ones, while the dangers inherent in spiritual individualism are more immediate and pressing. If your reason for avoiding institutional religion is the fear of the Inquisition or the Salem witch trials, or even just the stifling atmosphere of some pre-Vatican II Catholic parishes or Protestant small towns, you are letting a danger that's increasingly remote push you away from the things that are necessary to mitigating today's perils, today's problems—isolation rather than pharisaism, narcissism rather than authoritarianism, a world that leaves you alone in your despair rather than a society that's always nosing in your business.

Because it doesn't matter how sincerely you intend to seek the Tao, the knowledge of God, the true and righteous path. Without friendships, without social networks, without pastors or rabbis or teachers, without examples of other people striving as you are, without some form of support and advice and reassurance, any attempt to be religious is much more likely to collapse or wither on the vine.

## Not Every Door Should Be Opened

Or go badly, badly awry. This is the last but not the least reason to prefer religious commitment to spiritual dilettantism, to prefer an existing tradition to your own experiments: traditions and institutions offer spiritual protections that aren't available on your own. If the supernatural is potentially real it is also potentially dangerous, with more substantial stakes than most interactions in the natural and the everyday. Part of the point of the evolved technology of organized religion is to provide safety and security to travelers in this landscape—to connect the seeker to cosmic powers that are friendly to the human race, to help discern the difference between experiences worth pursuing and roads best left untaken, and to provide direct protection against the forces and experiences that seem destructive and demonic.

"Don't mess around with demons" might seem like too basic a message to require the structure of an entire religion to convey and reinforce. But in fact what happens in horror movies—the people who *go in that room* or *open that book* or *hold that séance* with predictably disastrous consequences—also happens in real life. Spend any time reading or talking to people working in the realm of experimental spirituality, whether they're just trying to open themselves to the universe, taking drugs to facilitate spiritual experiences, or dealing with some kind of weirdness they haven't consciously sought out, and you'll hear consistent stories about "encounters with negative entities," and consistent uncertainty about what to do about them. "Welcome the demon, expel, or ignore?" asked a recent post by a psychedelic practitioner, and clearly it's an open question for many people practicing experimentally, exploring solo on the fringe.[4]

For some, a small but meaningful minority, welcome is the straightforward answer, and if you're setting out to discover Satanism, then you probably aren't going to be talked into joining a more mainstream faith without some hard experience first. But other spiritually open-minded people experience a chronic uncertainty about how to handle negative encounters. And the mere appearance of the dark or negative or devilish, no less than the appearance of a ghost or monster in the horror movie, isn't by itself enough to convince them not to keep opening doors and looking into basements and wandering down corridors that might be better left unexplored.

Some religious traditions lay down absolute strictures against certain kinds of spiritual adventuring, others allow for more mystical curiosity, and there are different theological ideas about what different kinds of supernatural encounters mean. But no tradition encourages wandering mystic roads alone. Even the Amazonian shamans using ayahuasca to enter what they believe to be realms of real supernatural power operate in a spirit of self-protective caution, more like soldiers going on a mission than wanderers expecting peace and love and understanding. And unless you intend to train as a shaman yourself, assuming that your own resources suffice for self-protection is like setting out into a wilderness, not just without a reliable map, but without any defenses against the predators that might be waiting in the dark.

It's not only in the flatly negative experiences that you might want some trusty guides and useful rubrics and hard-earned ancient wisdom. Just because a spiritual experience feels positive, empowering, *amazing* doesn't mean it's always good for you, any more than any experience of bodily pleasure is necessarily nourishing or healthy. If you stipulate the existence of unfriendly spiritual powers there's no reason to assume that they would always appear as enemies or threats. Likewise, if you stipulate the existence of neutral or inscrutable spiritual powers, there's no reason to assume that a relationship with them couldn't change from positive to negative on their terms, rather than yours. And if you stipulate the existence of spiritual powers that have your good in mind, even a loving God who desires your glorification, there's no reason to assume that the journey toward sainthood would be one positive experience after another, rather than a mixture of raptures and dark nights of the soul, rewards and testings.

So you want to be able to test your own spiritual encounters against some accumulated wisdom and experience, to subject your private revelations to some kind of serious scrutiny, to find guides and maps even when you're enjoying the views that the road has opened up. In the ample literature on how intense spiritual experiences transform people, what's consistent is the change in belief—the newfound confidence in supernatural realities, the waning of certain kinds of existential angst, the ebbing of the fear of death. What's less consistent is the moral arc: the mystic may become a better person but it's not a guarantee, narcissism can replace despair as a chief temptation, an absolute confidence in one's own private revelations can overwhelm modesty and common sense, and other people's response to your mystical experience may encourage you to embroider future ones or simply make them up.

You don't even have to believe in hostile or deceptive powers to take these dangers seriously. You just have to believe in the human capacity to misinterpret, seek attention, and become addicted to certain experiences or certain powers that their visions seem to grant. It's part of normal human nature to take positive experiences and turn them into long-term negatives by letting pride and ego play, so of course it's a danger in the supernatural realm as well.

And the fact that some people who have notable religious experiences end up not as holy saints but as power-hungry gurus or self-aggrandizing messiah figures doesn't prove the initial experience was fraudulent or infernally inspired. Just as you can do the wrong thing with the life God or the Universe has granted you, it's entirely possible to do the wrong thing with a God-given experience—which is one reason the Catholic Church, in its attempts to validate supernatural encounters, doesn't assume that if one reported vision is heaven-sent then any claimed vision from the same source must be real as well.

"Saints should be judged guilty until proven innocent," George Orwell once remarked, and that spirit informs how institutional religion usually treats the more extreme forms of mystical experience—testing them, scrutinizing them, examining them against existing doctrine and prior revelation, and generally trying to keep the mystical personality tethered to humility and reality.

Just as the moralizing side of institutional faith can shade into a hypocritical conformism, the scrutinies inflicted on mystics can take suspicion to a punitive extreme. Hence the many tales of visionary saints unjustly persecuted by religious authorities in their lifetimes, their holiness accepted only after death.

But you do not inhabit sixteenth-century Spain; you inhabit a society whose errors run to the opposite extreme, toward an open-mindedness that makes every person their own shaman, that judges authority as guilty until proven innocent and treats the individual experience as the highest law of life. So yes, do not try to protect yourself from spiritual dangers by immediately finding the most restrictive spiritual community available. But do take your own limitations and fallibility seriously, do take the human need for community and correction seriously, do take the wisdom of evolved traditions and technologies as seriously as you take your own thoughts and feelings, and do take danger in the spiritual realm as seriously—no, more seriously—than you would take danger anywhere else. Do all this, and you will find yourself impelled away from dilettantism, away from do-it-yourself religion, and toward membership and belonging and submission, tempered by whatever uncertainties and reasonable doubts, in a tradition larger and older than yourself.

But which tradition, you ask? Let's take up those choices next.

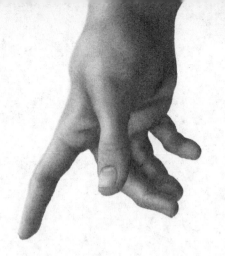

5

# Big Faiths and
# Big Divisions

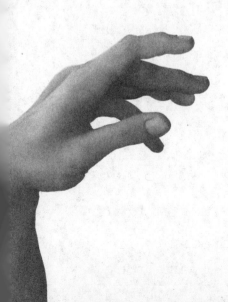

My parents ate health food in the 1980s, in the days before it was an upper middle class default—before Whole Foods and ubiquitous vegetarianism, when Asian cuisine in most American cities meant greasy Chinese takeout and organic produce was a specialty market rather than a normal section of the supermarket. To seek out even a veggie burger in those days required entering a subculture as exotic in its way as any charismatic healing service. So it made complete cultural sense that the vegetarian restaurant we visited most often, a storefront setup in Middletown, Connecticut, had an attached bookstore that mostly sold religious books and spiritual objects, with a New Age vibe, but no regard for doctrinal consistency. You could find crucifixes as well as crystals, Christian mysticism alongside astrological charts, texts from Islam and Buddhism and Judaism sharing shelf space with Transcendentalism and New Thought and Christian Science.

Having wandered happily in that bookstore after a flavorless meal, I can understand why someone might freeze up or feel entirely overwhelmed at being told they need to select just one shelf or display case, one set of books or one particular selection of religious objects, to organize their views about the cosmos.

It isn't just the issues discussed in the last chapter—the attractions of spiritual individualism, the fear of submission to a potentially abusive authority—that keep people hanging around the Bookstore of All Religions. I was already a believing Christian when I browsed through the Buddhist self-help and the Judaica, the copies of *A Course in Miracles* and *Women Who Run with the Wolves*, and I had no desire to create my own entirely personalized faith, no toxic experience of institutional religion to escape. But I still found it pleasant, at age twelve or thirteen, to just hang around a space where all the world's religions were on an equal footing—mostly, I suspect, because I was already aware that outside that space, in the world of the secular meritocracy, my religious beliefs were a curiosity. Whereas inside the bookstore, there was safety in numbers. Everyone was on the same side against the materialists, and surely all these different faiths together couldn't be wrong.

One faith alone, though, one faith claiming to be truer than the rest—well, that makes you a bit lonelier, a bit more vulnerable, and maybe uncomfortably close to the atheists in your determined rejection of all those other religions, all those rival shelves and icons.

Certainly that's what some atheists would have you believe. "We are all atheists about most of the gods that humanity has ever believed in," Richard Dawkins has argued. "Some of us just go one god further."[1] The idea behind this aphorism is that every serious religious worldview is a closed system, and that to really believe in one—to cease to dabble, to actually practice and believe—is to necessarily reject all the rest as incredible and false, on the same terms that materialists like Dawkins reject all forms of religious belief.

Our old friend David Hume made a similar argument: "In matters of religion," he wrote, "whatever is different is contrary; and that it is impossible the religions of ancient Rome, of Turkey, of Siam, and of China should, all of them, be established on any solid foundation."[2] In other words, since there are so many different religions across the world and human history, so many innumerable gods, if you think 99.9 percent of them were imaginary, the odds are good that your own preferred deity is imaginary as well.

Even if it doesn't convert you to atheism, this theory of the case creates a problem for the religious searcher. With so many different options, so many deities and faiths and churches, if you choose between them aren't you all but guaranteed to get it wrong? Especially under modern conditions, with all the religious variety on offer under pluralism. Maybe you should bet on God even if you aren't sure of His existence, but how could you possibly be expected to choose between all the different varieties on offer just within, say, Presbyterianism, let alone across all the religions of the world?

## True Faiths and True-Ish Faiths

Fortunately for the sincere seeker, Dawkins and Hume overstate their case. The Bookstore of All Religions isn't necessarily a library of total falsehoods with a few reliable exceptions scattered here and there. It is not true that religious claims are all simply exclusive of one another, or that to believe in one revelation, one conception of the divine, requires believing that every other religion is made up.

For instance, you can believe in a specific revelation that fulfills or clarifies the human relationship with God, and also believe that prior to that revelation, or among people who have not yet received it, authentic spiritual experiences abounded even if they were incompletely understood. You can believe in an ultimate form of mystical experience, a highest conception of the Absolute, and also believe that the same Absolute manifests itself through many different supernatural personalities and local deities. You can believe that some of the gods that people serve are real but also dangerous or deceptive—that we're better off not worshiping them, but that they nonetheless participate in spiritual reality, offering mystical experiences to seekers and favors to their worshipers whatever their ultimate intent.

Suppose your religious quest begins with Hinduism, the most important polytheistic tradition in the world today. Does that mean that you are preemptively deciding that monotheists are all simply deluded, that their Jehovah or Allah is just a fiction or a myth, and that their moral systems and spiritual practices are all just awful mistakes or blind alleys? Not at all. The sincere polytheist might assume that the Old Testament God is one deity among many—perhaps a very important deity, at that—whose powers and significance were exaggerated by His adherents but whose deeds on behalf of His favored people were entirely real. Or alternatively the sincere polytheist might also be a kind of monotheist, interpreting the Hindu pantheon as a proliferation of personalized and localized expressions of a single ultimate divinity, and seeing Jehovah as a (limited, but hardly made up) way of personifying that divinity as well.

By the same token, the Christian convert need not believe that the gods of the Hindu pantheon are simply fake and polytheism just a fraud. The early Christians had varying interpretations of the Greco-Roman polytheism they were seeking to displace: paganism was sometimes seen as an anticipation of the Christian revelation, seeded with intimations of the fuller truth, sometimes as a manifestation of angelic "princes" that God had set over various tribes and peoples; and often as a form of demonic rule, the "powers and principalities" that Christ had come to overthrow.

None of these beliefs implied that worshipers of Zeus or Athena were praying to nobody or to nothing, that everyone was worshiping figments of their own imagination before Christianity came along. The pagans might be doing something good and incomplete, focused without full knowledge on the true God and His messengers, or something dangerous that subjected them to powers in rebellion against heaven. But in either case they were participating in actual spiritual realities, performing acts that had real spiritual effects.

Similarly today's seeker, looking out across a diverse religious landscape, doesn't need to assume that there exists one lonely truth, potentially so tucked away and hidden that most searchers are doomed to wander perpetually in realms of utter falsehood. Rather the seeker should assume that there exist less-true and more-true schools of thought, and that they're looking for the tru*est* religious school within a continuum where many options have some validity, some connection to the ultimate reality being sought. Which means that even if you start in a wronger-than-average place you can still draw closer to your eternal destiny by conforming yourself to whatever that tradition still gets right. And if you never reach the absolutely truest place, you might still make a kind of progress, orient your life more closely to its cosmic purpose, or do something pleasing to the gods or God.

Let's call this the Emeth principle, after a character in C. S. Lewis's Narnian novels. Emeth is a devout adherent of the religion of Tash, a vulture-demon, who ends up being welcomed into heaven on the grounds that in performing works of virtue he has served the true god of Narnia, the lion Aslan, without knowing it—much like the sheep in Matthew's gospel, some of whom are welcomed into paradise because in helping the poor and sick and suffering they served Christ unawares.

This principle does not presume that all religions are basically identical, that nobody ever suffers for spiritual errors, that there is no possibility of condemnation, no scenario where any soul is ever lost. Certainly it was not a matter of indifference to Lewis whether people worshiped Aslan or Tash, and he wasn't implying that worshiping a fallen angel leads everyone to paradise.

The idea, rather, is that if some kind of God exists and ordered the universe for human beings, then even a false or flawed religion will probably contain intimations of that reality, signposts for the discerning pilgrim, some kind of call to higher things—such that a sincere desire to find and know the truth can fail to reach truth's fullness and still find its reward.

As with other arguments in this book, the Emeth principle makes the most sense if you assume that the universe is not some kind of conspiracy against true knowledge or belief, and that the landscape of religious belief isn't just a vast scheme of entrapment, where almost every tradition and sect leads inexorably to the dark. Rather, just as we should provisionally trust the evidence for design and order, the readily available supernatural intimations, we should provisionally trust that some access to divine purpose is widely available, and that many human beings and societies have found pathways that take you some distance toward the truth.

Which doesn't mean that you just sign up for the next vulture-demon cult that shows up at your doorstep, or cast your soul into the hands of any guru whose books happen to temporarily adorn the bestseller table in the Bookstore of All Religions. Instead you should start the way you would in any other area—by looking for wisdom in crowded places, in collective insights rather than just individual ones, in traditions that have inspired entire civilizations, not temporary communities. Even if you can't know for certain which road leads closest to the truth, you can still assume that the better trodden a religious pathway, the more wisdom there is in following after the generations that have trodden them before.

## The Case for the Big Religions

If this sounds like an argument that the more popular, enduring, and successful world religions are more likely than others to be true—yes, that's exactly what I'm arguing.

Of course this can't be true at every moment of history. If a new revelation or breakthrough suddenly arrives there will be a moment where the truest faith will be one of the smallest, where the stone the builder rejected is suddenly planted as a cornerstone for something new. A Christian is obliged to believe that the truest faith was held by just a few hundred people in the year 34 AD, a Muslim to believe the same about Muhammed's initial following, and it's always possible that the truest faith in the year 2034 is held by a handful of disciples gathered in a barn outside Toledo.

But even in the biblical image of the rejected stone, the promise is that a big new temple is going to go up, not that the stone will sit forever lonely in the field, worshiped in its grass-covered abandonment by a handful of initiates. If a faith claims to be much truer than the competition, if it represents a spiritual great leap or a breaking-in of divine wisdom into history, it's reasonable to expect proof of those qualities to emerge on a reasonable timeline, to see the effects of the breaking-in on the full sweep of human history, not just on a handful of human lives.

So in exploring faiths as a religious novice, it makes sense to start with religions where those effects are already manifest, where there's no question that the faith has historical significance and staying power. I'm not saying that you should ignore the divine call if you have a radical experience of the divine through a start-up Californian religion or an obscure sect from Dagestan; if you find God somewhere, it's only reasonable to assume that's the place God wants you to begin. But if you haven't found God, if you're just out there looking or trying to decide what sort of searcher to become, it's a reasonable bet that the big, resilient, long-enduring faith traditions— Christianity and Islam, Hinduism and Buddhism—are more likely to stand in a strong relationship to the truth about existence than religions that flared and died, that subsist in cultural isolation, or that came into existence the day before yesterday.

Especially since those big traditions have a certain amount of commonality, a number of shared premises, a certain degree of convergence notwithstanding their important differences. These convergences are not just in the realm of mystical practice or the "peace, love, and understanding" department that modern religious liberals tend to emphasize; they include shared ideas about more unfashionable concepts, from sexual morality and asceticism to demonic powers and the reality of hell. But taken together they suggest a story of development in human religious understanding, where the big religions came into existence, won converts, and spread around the globe because they represented a shared advancement in theological and moral understanding, an ascent toward more coherent worldviews and greater proximity to truth.

The ascent starts from what seems to be the natural religion of humanity, common to tribal societies on multiple continents and cultural contexts. This original faith treats divinity as an intensely immanent force, manifest in local deities, nature spirits, the ghosts of your ancestors, your own spirit, and the collective spirit of the tribe. Such natural religion also usually posits a kind of creator god or divine pantheon—but it isn't usually the primary object of practice and belief.[3]

Then, as tribal cultures give way to urban cultures and then to kingdoms and empires, another stage develops. First, in popular religion, there is a stronger emphasis on higher gods, who become associated with more complex forms of political order, such as the ancient god-king or the cult of the ancient city-state. At the same time in philosophical religion you see a movement toward more transcendent conceptions of divinity, where whatever high gods or divine principle governs the universe is more important, more real, perhaps more worthy of worship, than ancestral spirits and minor deities.

Subsequently, various leaders and visionaries and religious geniuses emerge to take these movements further, to combine trends in popular and philosophical religion, creating what we now think of as the major world religions, faiths that transcend city and empire as well as tribe and family. This process encompasses both the "Axial Age" described by the religious scholar Karl Jaspers, the period from the eighth century to the third century BC which saw the emergence of Buddhism, Taoism, the Hindu Upanishads, Zoroastrianism, Greek Platonism and the Judaism of the prophets, and then the subsequent appearance of Christianity and then Islam as missionary religions that remade the entire world.

The religious systems that emerge from this change share several key features. Local forms of divinity are more clearly subordinate to higher powers, which are seen as the most reliable source of moral guidance and spiritual protection. Human religion, ritual and moral practice, refocuses toward more transcendent goals, toward an ultimate destiny somewhere outside the material world as we know it: in eternal salvation, escape from material illusions, union with God or the Tao or ultimate reality, freedom from the wheel of reincarnation, nirvana. The natural world becomes partially disenchanted, perceived more as a system set in motion and governed by divine laws rather than one sustained constantly by supernatural action.

And human agency is more important. A fuller recognition of the true God or highest reality sets people free, to some degree, from the power of local spirits, the burdens inherited from their tribe or city or ancestors.

This is a very crude account, obviously, and each of the major world religions tells a different story about salvation, strikes a different balance between the forces just described—between God and human beings, nature and supernature, ultimate spiritual reality and immanent supernatural forces. But there is nonetheless a pattern in the making of these faiths, a balancing of the older emphasis on immanence with a desire for clearer moral guidance and eventual transcendence.

Seen from a secular point of view, this story is often usually folded into a larger narrative of long-term disenchantment. First we went from local gods to high gods and from pervasive mysticism to more bounded and limited supernaturalism, from human beings as prisoners of a spiritual ecosystem to human beings as freer agents who are merely influenced by spiritual realities. Then from the Middle Ages through the nineteenth century we gradually went further, pushing God into the role of a distant watchmaker. And from there it was a simple matter to do away with the God hypothesis entirely.

Not surprisingly I have a different perspective: I think the process whereby we moved from localized religion to the world religions was in fact a movement toward greater understanding and wisdom, while the (partial, incomplete) abandonment of those religions has been the late-modern world's great mistake. Rather than just being a way station on an unstoppable march from pervasive supernaturalism to disenchanted secularism, the great religions represented—and still represent!—a balancing that comes much closer than either modern materialism or primeval religions to capturing the full story of the world.

So if you are a seeker on the threshold of religion, a browser in the Bookstore of All Religions, it's entirely sensible to let yourself be drawn toward a major world religion rather than fretting that religious truth might be hiding from you in some minor Californian sect or exotic mystery cult. These religions spread around the world for a reason, they're available to you for a reason, they triumphed over primeval belief systems for a reason, they have moral and metaphysical commonalities for a reason—and that reason is that they represented an advancement, a convergence, toward a truer picture of reality.

But the convergence also has its limits. If you take the big faiths seriously as evolved structures, you shouldn't assume that their differences just vanish when seen from the correct God's-eye perspective. Rather, you should assume that the questions that divide them—both from one another, and internally—reflect important, reasonable divisions in how human beings might approach religion. In which case the best way to move from a narrowing of options to an active choice is take the dividing questions seriously and let your provisional answers guide your quest.

## Moral Guidance or Divine Experience?

Let's discuss a few dividing questions and their implications. The first division starts with a reaction that some readers may have had to the first three chapters of this book: a definite sympathy for the arguments about divine design and human exceptionalism, maybe a limited interest in the mystical as a category of subjective human experience—but a strong recoil from the wilder stuff, the angels and demons and cancer cures and broken radios transmitting from the great beyond.

It's possible to have a religious worldview that basically relies on this mix of responses—that accepts the possibility of a providential plan working itself out in human history but finds miracles to be just a bit too much, that regards divine intervention and special revelation as a kind of offense against the radical otherness of God, and that assumes that the point of being placed in this world is to do good and become good *in this world* without constantly trying to commune with invisible spirits or hurl oneself into some altogether different plane.

Then again it's also possible to have a perspective that insists that the wilder stuff is the whole point of serious religion, that if a faith system is mostly just a guide to the good life, then it doesn't have enough to offer to a suffering and struggling humanity, that allegory and symbolism in religious texts is interesting only if there's something completely literal there as well. For religion to matter, from this point of view, it can't just be a method of making yourself or the world a little bit more whole; it needs to supply both everyday enchantment and some hope of radical divine intervention. "Nothing can save us that is possible," wrote W. H. Auden. "We who must die demand a miracle."[4]

The closer you are to the first perspective and the more comfortable you are within its limits, the more it makes sense to embrace a religious tradition that emphasizes human ethical action over and above supernatural experience. In the Western world that could mean the liberal forms of Protestantism, with their hesitancy about miraculous claims and their zeal for social and political reform. It could also mean a Westernized form of Buddhism, of the kind eloquently presented in Robert Wright's recent bestseller *Why Buddhism Is True*, in which the gods and miracles and hungry ghosts of popular Buddhist piety are minimized and the practice of meditation is presented primarily as a tool for achieving personal and social harmony, for living happily and humbly and virtuously in this world, rather than encountering something wild and wholly Other.

But a certain caution around mystery and miracle isn't simply a liberal perspective. The more austere forms of Reformed Protestantism, for instance, accept that miracles are possible, but they tend to minimize their relevance for contemporary Christians—for instance by suggesting that certain forms of divine intervention ceased after the time of Jesus and His apostles. They also deemphasize the mystagogic element in religious practice generally, preferring simplicity in worship over anything that seems too eager for enchantment. Likewise conservative forms of Islam often stress a simplification of religion, a refusal of anything that seems too mystical or supernatural, an emphasis on simple obedience to the law as the truest form of faith— joined to an insistence on God's absolute otherness that makes even the representation of the divine unnecessary or blasphemous.

On the other hand, if you start from the perspective that the wilder side of religion is essential to its purpose, if you have a desperate hunger for spiritual experience and a sense that religion is either empty or implausible without some direct and personalized proof that God or the Universe cares intensely about *you*, then you aren't going to be happy with austere worship, therapeutic meditation, or detailed legal codes. You're going to want the promise of a sudden, enveloping personal encounter—the kind of promise offered especially in the charismatic and Pentecostalist forms of Christianity that have won so many people away from more buttoned-up and antisupernatural churches in the last hundred years. Or you'll want the sort of strenuous religious practices described by T. M. Luhrmann, the religious anthropologist whom we last met with the batteries melting her backpack, as "kindling the presence of invisible others"[5]—something that's usually the work of intentional, selective communities inside larger forms of faith.

Or maybe you're somewhere in between the two perspectives: open to mystery and miracle but not desperate for it, content with intimations of the numinous rather than more dramatic raptures, interested in a faith that delivers a certain dose of mysticism consistently but in a ritualized rather than personalized form. This is the religious mood that many forms of traditional liturgy and popular piety evolved to satisfy, whether in Roman Catholicism and Eastern Orthodoxy, Sufi Islam or Tibetan Buddhism. They promise transcendence through collective practices—mass and sacrament, smells and bells, prayer and festival—that aim to make human life feel permeable to divinity, without trying to somehow guarantee a personal encounter or ravishment.

Let's call these three approaches to religion the ethical, the experiential, and the liturgical. As described, they cut across the great traditions, and each one might just be a starting place. The person who begins by regarding religion as a guide for moral action and internal harmony might find themselves surprised by mysticism or miracle. The person who starts out as an intense experiencer might find their way eventually to a liturgical expression of their faith. But the starting place is what we're interested in here—finding the most natural doorway into a serious religion, and discovering where the path leads next.

## God or the Gods?

Now let's consider a question that separates the major traditions: Whether to worship the Absolute as one god or as many. Polytheism or monotheism? Multiple deities or one singular Almighty? The Abrahamic religions or the crowded pantheons of popular Hinduism and Buddhism?

Monotheism in some form has often tended to be the destination of philosophically minded believers. Once you accept that the universe is actually a fashioned thing, that human beings are meant to be here, that spiritual no less than physical realities exist and represent some kind of interface between eternity and the created timebound world, it seems intellectually natural to assume that there has to be some unity to the originating Mind, some single principle or Person at the heart of things.

Part of the convergence of the great religions is a convergence toward some version of "classical theism," some idea of a creating

God outside of space and time. This isn't just the position of the Abrahamic faiths; it also recurs as a potent philosophical idea in the various schools of Hinduism, competing with and overlapping with more pantheistic ideas about what the God-principle of Brahman represents. And even in Buddhism, the most non-theistic of the major faiths, you arguably see development toward more theistic conceptions of divinity over time. In Mahayana Buddhism, especially, the increasing divinization of the Buddha converges to some degree with Western ideas about a creator God, and the idea of the Buddha's "three bodies"—one earthly, one heavenly, one entirely transcendent—bears some not-entirely-distant resemblance to Christian ideas about the Holy Trinity.

But in their popular practice both of the major Eastern religions remain polytheistic. And there is an enduring case for polytheism even if you find monotheism philosophically compelling —namely, that the God of classical theism is just too distant, too absolutely Other to exist in a real relationship with timebound human beings. To have that kind of relationship, whether it takes the form of moral guidance or mystical experience or answered prayers, you need secondary forms of divinity that are more inside the world. Maybe, as in many schools of Hinduism, the gods are subordinate powers or manifestations or incarnations of Brahman—different timebound presentations of a timeless Oversoul. Maybe, as in some Buddhist schools of thought, they're all part of a self-sustaining and eternal cosmos rather than its omnipotent Maker, and thus even at their most powerful are limited in the same way as human beings. But in either case they are beings or manifestations unto themselves, and therefore legitimate centering points for worship and ritual and prayer.

In his 2016 book *Pagans and Christians in the City*, Steven Smith argues that even at its strongest, Western Christianity never fully did away with the desire for this kind of immanent, in-the-natural-world encounter with divinity, which endured in European folk religion and resurfaced in Renaissance hermeticism, in nineteenth-century occultism, and in the 1970s New Age.[6] The convinced polytheist might go farther and argue that *of course* these tendencies have re-appeared, because secondary powers are real and in some form their worship is natural and inevitable. Thus Islam announces that God is one, but its adherents are praying to local saints and pondering djinn and angels soon enough. Evangelical Christians denounce idol-atry but often end up talking about Jesus like a really good friend or neighbor or a boyfriend. Roman Catholicism claims to reject a pantheon of gods even as it posits both a God-man who brings the Absolute down to earth and a sinless mother who ascends to rule in heaven.

There are two monotheistic responses to this argument: one (more Protestant, Muslim, and Jewish) that acknowledges that theists can slip back into polytheism while insisting that it's essential to resist that slippage by rooting out idolatry; another (more Roman Catholic and Eastern Orthodox) that argues that good monotheists can acknowledge secondary powers without divinizing them, praying *with* the saints rather than to them, recognizing angelic and demonic powers without giving them inappropriate forms of worship.

The debate is worth highlighting because while skeptics of reli-gion have tended to treat paganism as especially anachronistic or absurd, in twenty-first-century America it seems a bit more like the coming thing. The forms it takes are sometimes pantheistic rather than overtly polytheistic, following Ralph Waldo Emerson and the Gaia hypothesis and James Cameron's *Avatar* in treating the natural world as an immanent revelation in its own right. But increasingly post-Christian spirituality features a strong interest in secondary powers that are actually personified. Self-conscious neo-pagans and Wiccans are trying to cast spells, summon spirits, and speak once more with pre-Christian gods. Psychedelic seekers are communing with the spirit guides who await at the end of their hallucinogenic quests. UFO enthusiasts portray alien races as our spiritualized elder brothers, come to bring enlightenment and even immortality.

The artificial-intelligence industry has acquired a mystical fringe that interprets the quest to build a silicon god in spiritual as well as scientific terms.

Note, however, that these forms of polytheism have no general religious structure, no shared cultic rituals, few genuine traditions, and few real links to real pre-Christian practices. (Wicca's claim to connect to some unbroken tradition of witchcraft is mostly bunk.) As such, they fail many of the tests I set out in the last chapter, in terms of supplying spiritual community or moral discipline or simple safety.

That last point is especially important because on the surface this kind of post-Christian spirituality can seem so warm and welcoming and consumer oriented, a Gwyneth-Paltrovian bathtub of self-care, that it feels like the opposite of dangerous. But the peril of polytheism is linked to the source of its appeal: by positing supernatural forces that are linked to the natural world rather than fully outside or above, it delivers a kind of intimacy but also an inherent danger—because one thing that's clear about physical nature is that it's extremely perilous, filled with predators and traps, things that will kill you without thinking twice, and places to get near-permanently lost. Which is why the darkest forms of polytheism can get very dark indeed, treating the book of nature as a moral template and worshiping gods of strength and cruelty, as in Aztec human sacrifice and bloody Viking conquest. If you go looking for the face of God entirely in immanent forms and secondary powers, there's always a danger that you'll end up worshiping a demon.

The convinced monotheist will insist that this danger inheres in polytheism no matter what. But in polytheism's more developed and enduring forms you have more emphasis on what's *above* the local gods—the Buddha and the higher gods in Buddhism, Brahman and Krishna in Hinduism. You also have more emphasis on the dangers of the spiritual life in a crowded polytheistic cosmos. The funeral rituals of Hinduism, for instance, don't assume that reincarnation somehow makes the soul's journey to the afterlife and back a simple one; the unhoused soul is understood to occupy a position as potentially perilous as a human being let loose in a jungle, and prayer and ritual proceeds according to those stakes.

Whereas the popular forms of paganism in Western culture, infused with a therapeutic sensibility and a very American style can-do optimism, feel much more fundamentally naive about what kind of terrain they're encouraging people to navigate. So if you're one of those seekers who finds the polytheistic idea attractive, while the God of monotheism seems too distant or hypothetical or alien for worship, you're probably better off looking to the east.

## What Are the Eternal Stakes of a Human Life?

The mention of Hindu funeral rites brings us to a third notable divergence—between religions that believe that this life is a singular and decisive drama and those that assume it's just one act in the larger story of your soul, one way station among many on the journey toward eternity.

To be clear, this does not mean that some great religions believe in heaven and hell and some do not. The consensus on the afterlife is worth emphasizing: in both East and West, under monotheist and polytheist premises, your choices in this life matter immensely to your subsequent destination; there are heavens and hells and realms in between; and how you live today helps determine what becomes of you when you enter those undiscovered countries. Across different faiths there is also a widely shared understanding of the afterlife as a kind of journey—through purgatory to heaven, further up and further in toward God, or through a transitional spiritual plane like the Tibetan Buddhist "bardo" on the way toward some form of rebirth. In some traditions the final destination is predetermined by your earthly life; in others the journey includes its own opportunities and perils. But in all of them the soul can end up somewhere decidedly nonheavenly. Even in traditions like Buddhism that don't necessarily posit a creator God outside time and space, it's taken for granted that you can die and go to hell.

The question that divides the great traditions is whether you remain there. In Buddhism and Hinduism the hellish planes can be as horrifying as in any Calvinist fire-and-brimstone sermon; the difference is that the soul passes through them, experiences its karmic punishment, and then is eventually reborn, transmigrated into some other life. In some forms of Christianity and Islam there can be a similar passage, not into rebirth but into heaven, where the hellish zone is experienced as a temporary purgation. But while some believers in both faiths—especially among contemporary Christians—believe that the purgation will finally be temporary for everyone, this is not the orthodox assumption in either Christianity or Islam. Both assume that even in a redeemed and transfigured universe, some souls are cut off from God forever.

This doctrine raises the inevitable objections: How can a good God leave a single soul in hell forever, whatever their earthly sins? How can any merely temporal crime, however savage, justly yield eternal punishment? Even if you understand hell as a free choice of the damned soul, a place whose doors are locked on the inside, how could an all-benevolent, omniscient, and omnipotent God have brought those self-imprisoned souls into existence in the first place, knowing that they will spend eternity in some kind of torment?

Anyone who finds the idea of hell's eternity morally perverse, a group that I suspect includes many of our society's sincere religious seekers, will have an automatic attraction to the alternative conceptions of the afterlife: either the Hindu and Buddhist vision of reincarnation (which is shared, it should be noted, by certain schools of Judaism; monotheism and reincarnation are not incompatible), in which all punishments, however severe, eventually give way to some rebirth; or, alternatively, to the kind of universalism embraced by some Christians and Muslims in the past and an increasing number in the present, in which hell will ultimately prove to be a purgatory for everyone who enters it.

But it's important to recognize the alternative perspectives have their own knots and difficulties. Reincarnation may seem more merciful than eternal punishment, but combine it with the conceptions of an eternal or cyclical universe that often appear in Eastern spirituality and you can get something that seems pretty infernal in its own right: A system where the wicked are subject to hellish punishments and recurring memory-wipes as they cycle through their multiple lives isn't necessarily all that different from the eternal punishment envisioned in Dante's *Inferno*—except that under conditions of perpetual reincarnation, the soul who never rejects evil or reaches enlightenment would suffer eternally without knowing it, like the main character in Christopher Nolan's movie *Memento*, whose past disappears every few minutes. (The spiritual phenomena discussed in the third chapter includes people who claim memories of past lives, but if reincarnation exists, clearly that kind of continuity of self is the exception rather than the rule.)

A Christian universalism, on the other hand, raises the question of whether this life and this universe, which monotheism insists is the great stage for the great epic that God is writing, can really be all that significant in the end. If someone dies deep in their sins and is justly condemned to a (temporary) hell, and the entirety of their soul's journey to God is assumed to take place in some uncharted zone after our bodily existence is permanently over, then what exactly was the bodily existence for? At least reincarnation assumes a persistent importance to embodied life, in which sins that deserve damnation from one life might be plausibly made up for across multiple lives of charity and suffering and self-abnegation. But if the rehabilitation of the greatest sinners all happens offstage, somewhere in the realm of spirit, with God effectively rebuilding or recreating souls that rejected Him and then ushering them into paradise, then why was it so important to have souls born into a fallen material creation in the first place?

Jesus' parables stress how the repentant sinner is always welcomed no matter how late his repentance comes; the laborers hired at the last hour of the day get the same wage as those who worked from noon till night. One way to think about universalism is that the same principle applies in the realm of spirit—that even buried deep in some Dantean circle the soul can always turn back to God and find forgiveness. But the question is whether every soul *must* eventually do this in order to vindicate God's goodness and perfection, whether true freedom eventually has to yield a choice for God—or whether the same freedom that makes our ascent to God meaningful also has to leave open at least the possibility of a permanent separation.

That possibility, no less than the welcome for the late-repenting, seems to be emphasized and insisted upon throughout the New Testament. And the fact that Christian universalists spend so much time reinterpreting the meaning of certain gospel passages and translations of certain words testifies to the central reason why so many Christians still believe in some form of eternal damnation: not out of a specific attraction to the doctrine of hell or an abstract choice between different theories of the afterlife but out of a sense of obedience to Jesus of Nazareth.

Which brings us to what is perhaps the most important question for anyone choosing a religious path.

## How Does God Appear in History?

As noted above, it's possible to embrace a religious perspective in which God is really manifest our world only through the ongoing act of creation, and never sullies the system of the cosmos with miracles or special revelation. It's also possible to embrace a religious perspective in which divine activity is a kind of consistent background noise, which has different effects on different people but seems mostly consistent across cultures and civilizations. Religious experiences are always there, available if you seek them earnestly enough. Divine messages may be imparted to some and not to others, certain saints or gurus may deserve a special following, some religions may get closer to the truth about the universe than others, and the most enduring religions may converge on universal truths. But there is no single final revelation, no direct intervention inside history that answers a set of questions permanently or establishes a people or an institution as particularly favored or important.

Alternatively you can believe that there is real development in religious history, in which human beings are progressing in fits and starts toward greater enlightenment, with some form of salvation waiting at the end. But within that long evolution each great religious development is just a step that can be subsequently superseded; each great teacher or religious founder gets at part of the truth but not the whole. So any commitment you make should be, in its own way, provisional and open-minded. "Never put a period where God has put a question mark," runs the slogan of a kind of liberal Christianity that most embodies this perspective in our own day.

Or, finally, you can believe that God acts more decisively and permanently, and that the religious seeker should be looking above all for some kind of discontinuity in human history, some place of dramatic revelation in whose light both past and future should be interpreted. The Jews are the Chosen People. Krishna was the living avatar of the Supreme God. Jesus is the Son of God, the alpha and omega, the firstborn from the dead. Muhammed is the Seal of the Prophets. The Bible or the Qur'an is the sacred revelation. Buddha is the Enlightened One, the template for all who follow.

If you're open to this possibility, open to a decisive revelation or a specific paragon of religious virtue, then the preceding questions we've considered are downstream of the most important choice.

You don't just want to start at the end of things, comparing the systems that the followers of Jesus or Muhammed or Krishna have constructed to explain the revelation, and choosing between them based on how you respond to their theologies and teachings. You want to start with the claimed revelation itself—with the allegedly divine person, the allegedly sacred book, the historical credibility of the story, the immediate consequences of this supposed revelation for the world.

And again, following our rule that the universe isn't out to cheat you, you don't need to engage with every single person who has ever claimed divinity or read every single putatively holy text. Instead you can assume that the wisdom of the human past and the workings of Providence have elevated a smaller set of figures and texts for a reason, and try to encounter several of them seriously, as a reader and a student of history and a person open to direct experience of the divine. You don't have to pull every text off the shelves of the Bookstore of All Religions; the big books will do for a start.

If you have no strong and specific reaction to these encounters, if the stories all seem too similar in their strengths and too muddled or mythopoetic in their differences, the miracles either not credible or not proof of anything in particular, the claims of historicity implausible—well, then you can step back to the other questions and chart your path based on the general orientations of the great religions rather than their specific history.

But if you read the New Testament and find Jesus to be a remarkable figure and the Gospels shockingly credible as a historical narrative, if God speaks to you through the Bhagavad Gita or the Qur'an or the Pentateuch, if Buddha's teaching seems like the answer to all the riddles of your life—well, you should probably not then simply return to the more abstract questions, rejecting Christianity because you find polytheism more credible than monotheism or turning away from Hinduism because you don't really believe in reincarnation.

No: if there's any chance at all that you've found *the* place where God reached in or a great-souled human being reached up and out, then the theologies that developed from that revelatory moment should be given special weight even if you aren't fully persuaded by their details. And if you've never experienced belief before, if you feel yourself to have a completely open mind, and suddenly a specific text or figure leaps out at you, a story speaks to you like nothing else, then you should take the possibility that God is speaking to you very seriously; at the very least it's a strong signal that this is where you're supposed to start.

## The Paths between the Paths

Which does not mean that it will be the place where you should end. The key questions separating the major world religions are urgent and important, and obviously nothing separates them more than their claims about which teacher or prophet or sacred scripture is the highest thing or the essential word of God. But just as the different modes of religious practice can lead into one another—ethical religion becoming liturgical religion, mystical religion inspiring ethical religion—so too none of the great traditions are islands from which it's impossible to escape, or from whose shores no other continents are visible.

It isn't just that, contra Richard Dawkins, most religions allow for the possibility that other faiths are getting at least some things right—performing acts of worship or doing good works that aren't all simply in vain. It's also that any developed religious tradition will have places of overlap with its rivals that can be bridges outward, should you decide that your first commitment was mistaken or provisional and something deeper and truer is present somewhere else.

For instance, the place of Jesus Christ in Muslim theology is high enough that a Muslim might be drawn toward considering the truth of Christianity just through the sincere practice of Islam. Meanwhile the sincere Christian organizes their religious life around a story that, under Muslim premises, anticipates and finally culminates in Muhammed's revelation.

Likewise, even though Buddhism's initial vision of salvation does not include a classical-theist conception of God or Allah or Brahman, one can still find overlap between Buddhism and the more theistic great religions, especially in those modes of theology that approach God through negative statements, an emphasis on all the things that He is not. Meanwhile the moral teachings of the Buddha and Jesus of Nazareth have enough in common that a seeker could follow the Noble Eightfold Path toward the New Testament without feeling like they have to strike out through some vast wilderness to get there.

Or again, the Christian emphasis on God's presence in His creation is quite different from polytheism and pantheism, but not so different as to make those kinds of beliefs unintelligible. The choice between transcendence and immanence matters, but there is a sense in which all serious religion is trying to either discern the transcendent in the immanent, or else wrestle something that seems transcendent, like Jacob struggling with the angel, into something that we can hear or serve or understand.

In Christianity's debates about what constitutes heresy or orthodoxy, one recurring idea is that a heresy is not exactly a simple error but instead a truth that's gotten away from other truths and ended up overemphasized at their expense. My suspicion is that when humankind no longer sees through a glass darkly, when arguments between theists and pantheists or Muslims and Christians or Buddhists and Hindus give way to resolution, we'll be able to say the same about many of the world's great religions—that if they erred it was in taking some important truth too far, emphasizing some real attribute of God or the Universe but falling short of the full synthesis, maintaining as a secondary teaching what turned out to be primary instead.

This makes the argument between them essential, not something just to be papered over. We should want the full synthesis, the truest balancing of insights, the controlling revelation if such a thing exists. But the existence of secondary themes and internal tensions within faiths, and ideas and patterns that overlap across them, should grant some confidence to the seeker that just by choosing one faith and practicing it, they will probably get closer to the truth than if they hover forever in agnosticism.

Your choice might be the wrong one ultimately but the right one for you in that moment, or the wrong one but with enough that's right in it to make an important difference in your life. And if, in the end, your initial conversion doesn't convert you to *the* true faith, the religion you enter will have hopefully acquired enough truth and wisdom in its long development to make a ladder upward, from the mire of meaninglessness and the snares of indecision toward whatever the full plan of your life is meant to be.

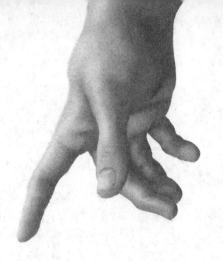

# 6

# Three Stumbling Blocks

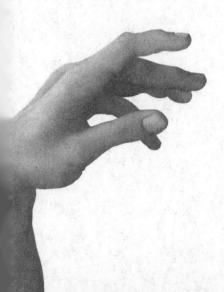

So far I have tried to present a case for religion that is more empirical than moral, stressing the good reasons to believe rather than suggesting that we need belief in order to be virtuous. Obviously I think that the existence of a cosmic order helps explain our moral intuitions and ideals, our sense of sin and shame when we fall short of our true or highest purpose, the development across the great religious faiths of an overlapping moral vision of how human beings should and should not act. But the existence of that order is a better argument for morality than morality is for the existence of a cosmic order.

"If there is no God, all is permitted," while true enough, cannot by itself be the primary reason to believe in God. Rather, we can be confident that all is not in fact permitted only once we recognize that God in some form almost certainly exists.

But in emphasizing empirical reasons to think that the divine is real and worth pursuing, I've left myself open to a moral critique of religion, and especially of the great traditions I spent the last two chapters insisting that the religious seeker ought to join. For many liberal-minded modern people, an intellectual default to disenchantment isn't the only obstacle to joining or rejoining the churches or mosques or temples where their ancestors once prayed. An ethical case against traditional religion looms large as well—a sense that arguments about the true nature of existence are all very well, but a decent person just can't accept the moral authority claimed by the major traditions, their priests and leaders, or their gods.

So let's take on three versions of that case, in the form of moral questions that the person on the threshold of belief might raise.

## Why Does God Allow So Many
## Wicked Things to Happen?

As much as any supposedly scientific case for strict materialism, many people see this question as the trump card for atheism, a fundamental reason to reject religious worship or belief. From the horror of the Holocaust to the horror of a child's death from cancer, from the wickedness of human beings to the natural disasters whose recurrence is built into the structure of the world, the question assumes that there is just too much suffering in this universe to believe that a good deity created it. Any actual existing God would resemble a North Korean dictator, in a famous Christopher Hitchens formulation, demanding slavish worship while he lets his subjects starve and die. If God is all-powerful, He cannot be all-good; if He is all-good, He is not all-powerful. Ergo, no such God exists.

This is a potent enough argument that religious believers have been wrestling with it since basically forever. The core text of Western theodicy, the book of Job, ends with God overmastering Job's challenge but also declaring him vindicated against the friends who insist on pat answers, a prosperity-gospel world where happiness and success are proof of virtue and suffering proof of sin. If God exists, He seems to want us to have this argument, not just with each other but with Him. So to raise the argument is to be in good company—with Job, with Abraham, with the psalmist, even with Jesus lamenting His own abandonment on the cross.

But to claim that the argument is easily settled against divinity, that it's such a slam dunk as to justify outright atheism and not just argument and doubt, is a pretty peculiar presumption.

To begin with, like the more confidently atheistic versions of the scientific project, the moral case against Almighty God assumes a version of the very premise it ostensibly denies—that human beings are so distinctively fashioned among all the creatures of the world that we are equipped to stand outside material creation and comprehend it so completely as to make a certain moral assessment of how good and evil are balanced or imbalanced in the cosmos. Indeed it assumes that we can identify good and evil as meaningful categories at all, as opposed to just flags of convenience for things we have to instinctively favor and dislike.

Because only such a presumption makes it possible to place any trust at all in humanity's ability to offer a serious objection to how an omnipotent God might have ordered His creation. If God existed and human beings were as certain materialists think we are—jumped-up apes laboring under an illusion of self-consciousness, our sense of free choice and intellectual "judgment" entirely ordered by our hormones and neurons—by what possible standard would we pass moral judgment on anything or anyone, much less the universe's Architect? None, of course. To make that moral judgment, to condemn God's moral failures, is to already assert something about human beings' stature and capacity that only a religious conception of the human person can seriously allow.

Then, too, some of the intensity of that moral judgment on God's failings seems very specific to a residually Christian culture, which even in its secularized form retains a sense that the truest morality has been fully revealed in the person of Jesus of Nazareth, His teaching and His example and His death. The doctrine of the incarnation is an arguable answer to the problem of evil—here is God Himself, answering our laments by coming down to share in all our sufferings and die in torture alongside us. But it's also an arguable intensification of the dilemma, since it makes God's goodness seem especially intimate and loving and embodied, complete with healings for the sick and special friendship for children and the suffering poor. If this is how intimately God loves us, why is there any evil in the first place? If this is what God does when He comes to earth, why in God's name can't He do it all the time?

But this is a problem that's specific and meaningful inside Christianity, something to wrestle with once you've already generally accepted the incarnation and the rest of Christian faith. Step back from the intimacy of the Gospels to monotheism's basic conceptual framework, in which an omniscient God creates, sustains, and deals out justice to beings—us—whose own existence is both impossibly contingent and yet also potentially eternal, and it becomes a bit harder to assert that you know better than this God about how even the worst hardships of a timebound human existence will look in the light of eternity.

It's true that there can be something arid and seemingly unfeeling about the philosophical claims made on behalf of the God of monotheism—for instance, that the possibility of profound suffering is simply necessary because human freedom is the greater good and to create a world without evil would require making us automatons. But to feel that this conception is too abstract and bloodless, that it misses the moral depth of the problem created by every dead child or bereaved parent, that something has to be missing from our understanding—all these sentiments are quite different from immodestly declaring the question settled, the case against God closed, when by definition He has the eternal perspective and you for the time being do not.

God's response to the complaints of the suffering Job, "Where were you when I laid the foundation of the earth?"[1] is not an argument ender, at least when it's delivered by a religious text rather than the voice of God Himself. But it is an argument, and an important one! And if you're sure that you have seen enough of the cosmos to know that a moral omnipotence couldn't have created this one, you need to recognize the remarkable scale of that presumption, the confidence that if an explanation escapes your timebound consciousness it must not exist.

But then let's suppose for the sake of argument that the presumption is correct: the problem of evil does away with either God's perfect goodness or God's omnipotent ordering of the universe; you have to choose one. In that case you still have not actually done away with the arguments for being religious. The ordering of the universe, the distinctive place of human consciousness, and the evidence for the supernatural all remain. And as we just discussed in the preceding chapter, it's perfectly possible to practice religion seriously without making the omnipotent God of classical theism the center of your worship.

You might take a view of divine power as something essential to the universe and responsible for various aspects of our lives, but not necessarily the cosmos's omnipotent and omniscient Creator—which would explain why the universe as a whole seems imperfect, and why there is no final way to transcend suffering that doesn't involve transcending existence itself.

You might think of God as a pantheistic spirit that's all-pervasive but not all-powerful in the sense imagined by the philosophers of Western monotheism. You might assume that He's a being who changes with and is changed by His creation, as in the so-called process theology that influences some liberal Christian thought. You might embrace the gnostic idea that the true God is outside and above a material universe that it did not personally create, sending messengers and interventions to help us escape from our cycles of suffering into a purer realm of spirit. You might think of God as the friendlier part of a dualist principle, in which good and evil and creation and destruction are intertwined like yin and yang.

In all of these cases and more, it would be odd indeed to say that if divinity isn't omniscient and omnibenevolent in exactly the sense that many religions and philosophers imagine, there's no point in interacting with the spiritual realm, trying to align yourself with higher powers, or otherwise behaving in a religious manner. Such a divinity could still be responsible for life and death, it could still offer some form of salvation or transcendence, and it could still be working to enlighten human beings, to offer them moral teachings, to prepare them for everlasting life. Before the rise of the great religions almost everyone believed in gods and spirits without imagining them to be perfect or omnipotent. Many of the higher gods of polytheism still match the above descriptions, and so do various heterodox interpretations of the Old and New Testaments. So even if you feel absolutely certain that classical theism or Christian orthodoxy is mistaken about God, you have still barely begun to reckon with religion.

Of course a less than perfect divinity could be working against us, not for us. It could be our jailer or our torturer, or some malignant Lovecraftian intelligence that created us and then mercifully forgot about us, and whose attention we should not wish to attract via worship or prayer or any other kind of outreach. This idea has a certain doomy appeal, a pessimistic frisson; it's the stuff of excellent horror fiction. But it's simply implausible as a complete picture of reality. Maybe you can plausibly convince yourself, if you sink deeply enough into late-modern despond, that the world and human life are on balance bad, that in the weighing out, the darkness too often wins over the light. But the idea that the light does not exist at all, that there is nothing good about the universe, nothing of love and saintliness and beauty, is refuted comprehensively in every single instant. And as long as there is something good in the natural world, then if the supernatural exists there must be something good in those realms as well—something that might appear weaker than Satan or Cthulhu in a given moment, but still has to be worth seeking out, reaching toward, aligning with even if it doesn't have quite as much power as some religions and their adherents might believe.

Finally we should be especially skeptical of a despairing perspective on existence that seems to gain power and influence, as pessimism has in our time, even as many of the physical evils that it most decries abate. If it can seem offensive for believers to quote justifications of God's goodness to people suffering through pain and trauma and bereavement, it also seems somewhat offensive for nonbelievers in a society like ours, with life expectancies lengthened, terrible diseases conquered, and wealth piled up beyond human imagining, to lecture the inhabitants of the more deprived and painful human past on the naivete of their greater religious faith.

It is not true that there are no atheists in foxholes or on sickbeds. Some people do fall into disbelief and despair in the face of suffering and death. But as a generalization, human beings facing terrible forms of suffering often have less trouble reconciling their experiences with a strong belief in God than people in rich, long-lived, relatively safe societies like ours—societies in which suffering somehow has come to seem more morally offensive the less we actually experience it.

The stronger belief of the suffering person or the death-haunted society may, of course, just be a coping mechanism, which health and wealth and stability should make us mature enough to set aside. But the argument against God's goodness rests, at its strongest, on a moral intuition rather than a perfect proof—a sense that certain forms of suffering are just too awful to be justified by any larger economy of salvation, any eternal settling of accounts. And if you're rejecting God on the basis of a moral intuition about the experience of suffering, it's a little ridiculous to simply wave away the fact that the vast majority of people in history who have directly experienced the worst have not shared your intuition, indeed have often rejected it entirely in favor of resilient belief.

Likewise with some of the divisions in experience in our own well-off time and place. Thanks to an unfortunate encounter with a tick-borne illness, I've spent much of the last decade living in both the successful and prosperous world of the Acela Corridor and the bedraggled, financially stressed, pain-wracked world of people who suffer from chronic ills that our medical system doesn't know how to cure. I don't think it will surprise you to learn that religious faith of various kinds—Christian, Jewish, pantheist, New Age, you name it—is far more prevalent in the realm of constant suffering than it is in the realm of prosperity and comfort. And when nonbelieving intellectuals insist they understand the problem of evil fully enough to reject religion outright, on the basis of experiences that don't usually yield atheistic conclusions among the people who are actually going through them—well, let's just say that it looks a bit less like a rigorous review of the evidence and more like the motivated reasoning of people who have the same reasons as the privileged in every generation to disbelieve in a judgmental God.

But the intellectuals have their own comeback: it's not just God you're asking us to believe in, it's religions and religious institutions. If aligning with religion is supposedly aligning with the weak and lowly against the powerful and privileged, then the next question pops up.

## Why Do Religious Institutions Do So Many Wicked Things?

If the case against God's goodness almost always references the Holocaust, this argument almost always references the Inquisition. Whatever the notional benefits of religious membership, how can one reasonably subject one's life and choices to institutions that are responsible for so much intolerance and bloodshed, so many benighted centuries of repression and persecution?

It is certainly true that the history of organized religion is steeped in wickedness and sin. It is also true that the history of every organized human activity is steeped in crimes and cruelties. The history of the family, the history of business and commerce, the history of politics and government, are all replete with dramas of cruelty and subjugation and abuse.

One might look at this history and conclude that human beings should therefore live somehow without families, without trade, without political relations—but this is a view for adolescents, hermits, and misanthropes. The normal view is to recognize the needs met by these institutions, the necessary work they do, the progress to which they can contribute, the truths they convey, and get on with the business of trying to make them better, less corrupt, the best version of themselves.

Thus the most radical critic of the many crimes committed by the government of the United States of America can tear up at "This Land Is Your Land" and feel a swell of patriotic hope when she casts a vote for Bernie Sanders for president. The most disillusioned child of a broken home can still fall in love and vow perpetual devotion. The person failed most by the medical system can still aspire to find a healer who can help them. And similarly, the most convinced critic of institutional religion's historical sins, even the person wounded in some deep way by a specific pastor or congregation, can still hope to find in the diversity of religious institutions a place of support and a ladder to transcendence.

But surely, comes the rejoinder, organized religion is in a special category of evil, for all the utterly pointless wars that it has started, all the senseless killing over minute metaphysical disputes that defined the world before secularism arrived?

"The most detestable wickedness," wrote Thomas Paine, "the most horrid cruelties, and the greatest miseries, that have afflicted the human race have had their origin in this thing called revelation, or revealed religion."[2] So why not let the institutions responsible for all that misery simply die off, and if we have spiritual needs seek some new means to satisfy them?

Here, I'm afraid, we are entering the realm of atheistic self-deception. There is no good evidence that religion has been a special source of violence in human history, as compared to the entirely worldly and secular aims of conquest or resource control that drive most warfare between countries and peoples. Nor is there evidence that religious belief generally makes wars bloodier or crueler than they otherwise might be. Certainly in specific cases the fanaticism of the devout has that effect, but it's easy enough to find examples where the pattern runs the other way, with religion fostering or influencing attempts to gentle war and restrain its participants.

Any society that takes religion seriously will, of course, look for theological justifications for its political decisions. But that's no different than noting that democratic countries tend to justify their wars as valiant struggles for liberty—sometimes credibly, sometimes cynically, often somewhere in between. Religious impulses, like other loves—home, family, freedom—are often exploited or suborned by worldly powers. But this is just as likely to reflect the unfortunate captivity of religious institutions to kings and would-be conquerors than the captivity of some kind of otherwise-peaceable secular politics to the bloodlust of religious zeal.

All attempts to measure the true causes of conflict are inherently a bit arbitrary, but a couple of figures are worth citing here, both drawn from an essay by the historian Andrew Holt on "The Myth of Religion as the Cause of Most Wars."[3] Holt first cites Charles Phillips and Alan Axelrod's three-volume *Encyclopedia of Wars*, an analysis of 1,763 wars spanning most of human history, whose authors attempt to categorize different kinds of conflicts based on their primary motivation: just 121 fall under the category of "religious wars." No doubt if you handed the same list to Thomas Paine he would categorize things rather differently, but at the very least it should sow some doubt about treating religion as a unique cause of bloodshed.

Likewise, an effort by Matthew White to compile a list of the one hundred worst atrocities in human history—a book described by Steven Pinker, by no means a great friend of religion, as offering "the most comprehensive, disinterested and statistically nuanced estimates available"—ascribes eleven of the hundred horribles on his list primarily to religion. As Holt notes in his essay, White somewhat mystifyingly places Aztec human sacrifice, one of the most Satanic of religious customs, in a different category, "human sacrifice," so 12 percent rather than 11 percent seems like the more appropriate takeaway from his research. But the general point is clear: conflicts like the Thirty Years' War or China's Taiping Rebellion that have religion as a primary cause, such that you can argue that they would not have happened absent some doctrinal dispute or messianic proclamation, are the exceptions in the history of human warfare, not the rule.

This should be especially clear from the history that followed after Paine's confident pronouncement, which undermined his sweeping condemnation of religion much as subsequent history undermined David Hume's pontifications on the mystical and supernatural. When Paine published his pamphlet blaming the Bible and Christianity for all the bloody wars of Europe, Napoleon Bonaparte was three years away from his accession as First Consul. Over the next two decades a set of wars fought (depending on your perspective) for the sake of his ambitions, France's interests, or the cause of political enlightenment left as many as five million Europeans dead. This was just a warm-up act for the great power wars and political persecutions of the twentieth century, which piled up tens of millions of casualties in the name of nationalism, Communism, and fascism—all causes untainted by the dogmas of revealed religion, and yet somehow, despite Paine's expectations, much more pitiless than the Christendom they overthrew.

This should be entirely unsurprising when you realize that the very idea of Christendom—a supranational entity making specific, detailed moral claims on all its members—is an example of how the great religious traditions have attempted to transcend the local, familial, and national loyalties that actually drive most human conflict. This was true in the Axial Age when the great religions began to take their modern shape, it was true when the Christian revolution overtook the Roman Empire, and it's been true for most of American history—in which Christianity, usually Protestant Christianity, has been the basis for the most insistent demands for racial equality and universal citizenship.

Indeed it is extremely strange for anyone who inhabits the current liberal order, with its framework of universal rights, its humanitarian ideals, its missionary impulses that sometimes work and sometimes come to grief, and think of themselves as lucky escapees from a world of religiously motivated politics. The entire order we inhabit is built upon many centuries' worth of attempts by people with religious impulses—often strong and strange ones—to gentle the great powers of the world, to force moral absolutes upon statesmen who preferred to deal in machtpolitik, to impose rules that were often, if not always, justified with appeals to a higher law, to heaven itself, to nature's God.

The idea of international law emerged from the work of Spanish Catholics and Dutch Protestants; the abolitionist movement was a work of Quakers and evangelicals; the Universal Declaration on Human Rights was written mostly by a Catholic. Mahatma Gandhi and Martin Luther King Jr. were not secular figures, whatever else they may have been; Abraham Lincoln's Second Inaugural Address is not a secular document; William Wilberforce and Bartolomé de las Casas invoked the Bible, rather than rejecting it, when they railed against the evils permitted by their supposedly Christian governments. Perhaps the structures of peacemaking built upon all of those religious efforts no longer need religious ideas to remain standing (though you know *I* think they do). But the idea that the modern world has been built simply in bold secular defiance of religious violence is more mythological than Zeus.

Let me make one concession, however, which might be useful to thinking about your own religious choices. If all the great religious traditions tend to see themselves, in some way, as gentling the evils of the world, restoring harmony between God and humans or human beings and each other, some are more likely to see that obligation as an inherently institutional and political one—requiring the use of worldly power, sometimes comprehensive legal power, for the sake of their good ends. This is true of Roman Catholicism relative to much of Protestantism; it's true of Lutheranism or Presbyterianism or Anglicanism relative to Anabaptist forms of Protestant belief; it's true of Islam in both its Sunni and Shi'a forms.

Leaning into the political and legal is a good way to achieve real things in the world, and these faiths often tend to think especially deeply about questions of political order. But because they are more likely to allow themselves to become intertwined with governments or assume political power in their own right, they are inevitably more tempted to abuse or misuse power. Most of the very real cruelties perpetrated in the name of religion emerge from this temptation, this comprehensivist impulse, whereas there has not been (to my knowledge) an Anabaptist inquisition. So if you have a special horror of the evils of persecution or theocracy, you may find it more natural to seek out religious traditions that define their own rules and boundaries in ways that rule those temptations out.

This refusal of power, this quietism, can overlap with the more liberal forms of religion, but it's not exactly the same thing, since often the liberal religious worldview also assumes an intensive political project, even as it tries to avoid granting much power to religious institutions themselves. Indeed, much of liberal religion sees itself in clear continuity with the political efforts I've just described, the long attempt to force kings and politicians to conform to religious moral codes. And its most important separation from traditional forms of faith isn't in an attitude toward politics, but an attitude toward the last of our stumbling blocks, the final question for this chapter.

## Why Are Traditional Religions So Hung Up on Sex?

Even more than the Copernican and Darwinian revolutions, the sexual revolution stands as the crucial cultural prop for contemporary unbelief. Since the upheavals of the 1960s, it's increasingly taken for granted by the average American or Westerner that a modern and enlightened person must reject the constraining sexual ethics of traditional religion, the prohibitions on premarital sex, divorce, homosexual relations, even nonprocreative sex.

Crucially it's not only Christian ethics that are rejected here but teachings found in all the great traditions, notwithstanding occasional portrayals of Buddhism and Hinduism as inherently more sexually nonjudgmental than the Abrahamic faiths. In reality, as Damien Keown writes in his introductory guide to Buddhist ethics, while Buddhist teaching on sexuality is not always as specific as in Western faiths, "Buddhism in general adopts a wary attitude toward sex," teaching that "control of the appetites and desires is a prerequisite for spiritual development," and emphasizing the virtue of celibacy over marriage and procreative over non-procreative sex.[4] Likewise, although Hinduism is rather famously open to the religious dimensions of sexual pleasure, within its various schools the consensus on premarital and extramarital sex is much closer to Christianity or Islam than to contemporary liberal norms.

For the post-sexual-revolution skeptic, it's not just that these older religious moral codes are seen as antiquated or deluded. They're often seen as actively perverse, rooted in misogyny and patriarchy and homophobia and a fearful puritanism, inflated by the ridiculous idea that the Architect of the entire universe would care about what consenting adults do with their genitals. So to join a faith tradition that still upholds a serious code of chastity is, from a certain contemporary point of view, to actively embrace *im*morality. From this perspective there isn't just the mystery of why God merely allows bad things to happen; there's the problem of God or sacred scripture or the institutions of the faith actively giving instructions that seem punitive and wicked. To bind yourself to such a community, in the way that I've been arguing you should—well, it doesn't matter what evidence for divine design there might be, you might as well apply for citizenship in Margaret Atwood's imagined Gilead.

The easiest response to this potent sentiment is to point out that if traditional sexual ethics are your only reason not to become religious, there is good news: plenty of religious believers agree with many of your objections to their own moral traditions, and many liberalized forms of religious faith stand ready to welcome you with open arms. In almost every major religious body extant in the developed world, extensive efforts have been made to revise and reinterpret all the teachings a modern person might find off-putting and offensive, sometimes completely changing the official institutional message, sometimes just carving out spaces where you can practice Catholicism or Islam without feeling judged for your divorce, your same-sex relationship, your abortion, your premarital sexual relationships.

Do you wish that Christian churches only emphasized Christ's teachings about helping the poor, or that synagogues only preached *tikkun olam*, the repair of the world, instead of fussing over people's gender roles and sex lives? If you inhabit any major US city you can find a church or synagogue that tries to do exactly that. Do you think the sexual revolution represented an essential ethical evolution that, if a good God exists, leaves liberal societies more in alignment with His (or Her) divine and holy will? This is also the current view cf Reform Judaism, parts of mainline Protestantism, various liberal and feminist reinterpreters of Islam, and more than a few people close to the current supreme pontiff of the Roman Catholic Church. Their shared worldview acknowledges that sexual morality is a unique stumbling block for the spiritual seeker of today—and then tries, as cleanly as possible, to simply remove the obstacle entirely.

In general these forms of religion have failed to attract as many people as the liberalizers expected, earning scorn from more con-servative believers for their demographic struggles. But you, the reader of this book, are not a demographic generalization or a sta-tistical average. If you find the general case for faith convincing but Islam's traditional attitude toward women retrograde or the Catholic Church's teaching on, say, masturbation ludicrous, then you should seek out the forms of religion that agree with you, build them up and let them try to build you up; become the change you seek in the religious world. If you resent religious institutions for taking an important message about life and death, an important source of connection to eternity, and an important source of community and fellowship, and binding it all to archaic rules about which sex can be ordained and which couples can be married—well, then you should consider joining those churches or institutions that agree with your critique.

Notwithstanding this exhortation, though, one good reason that social and cultural liberals don't rush the doors of their nearest progressive congregation is that rules about sexual morality aren't just incidental to the great traditions. They're woven deeply into their ideas and practices in ways that are harder to untangle than the liberalizers sometimes want to believe. It's possible to think that Christianity or Islam or any other faith is a locus of divinely revealed truth about the universe and that it's gotten sexual ethics almost completely wrong from the get-go. But there's a certain tension between those two beliefs, and it's hardly ridiculous to think that the second one substantially undermines the first. *Come worship the God who revealed Himself to us, and who, by the way, let us go completely and cruelly wrong about sex and gender for several thousand years* isn't an ideal pitch even if it seems to fit the spirit of the times.

Instead a reasonable seeker might say, *I can join a faith tradition that's made mistakes and perpetrated injustices, but I have to believe that its sexual ethic contains some real wisdom, some spark of divine insight, to have confidence in its worldview.*

So here are two related arguments to that effect, both stopping short of asking you to give up on every aspect of post-1960s culture.

First, the broad idea that what you do with your genitals doesn't matter to the condition of your soul—that any Supreme Being has better things to do than scrutinize your porn cache or police your lusts—is not nearly as intuitive as many modern people seem to think.

If you assume that God doesn't care about most people at all, that no individual life or relationship matters in the grand scheme of things, then sure, sex doesn't matter, but it doesn't matter because almost nothing else that we do matters either.

But once you accept that the universe was probably made with us in mind, that there is some cosmic purpose to human consciousness and human lives, then why *wouldn't* God or the cosmos care about the most important way that human beings bond with one another, create the most intimate and the most sprawling intergenerational forms of community, and participate in the creation of new life?

It would be a strange God indeed who cared intensely about how we spend our money or what votes we cast or how we feel about ourselves, but somehow didn't give a damn about behaviors that might forge or shatter a marriage, create a life in good circumstances or terrible ones, form a lifelong bond or an addictive habit, bind someone to their own offspring or separate them permanently. To the extent that this God is assumed to be preparing us for a life that transcends earthly existence, it would be especially strange not to care about how people approach one of the strongest desires of the flesh, the most embodied form of passion, the kind of carnal impulse that humans are most likely to glory in and also most likely to feel as a form of bondage.

You may think that the specifics of a traditional sexual ethic are misguided, in other words, but to think that a serious religion with a serious view of the human relationship to God wouldn't have a stringent sexual code of some kind is a bizarre assumption. If God cares about anything, He cares about sex; if any of your choices matter eternally, your sexual choices probably matter more than most. So in doubting the particulars of how the great religions approached sexual rules and sexuality, at least give them credit for having a more realistic view of sex than someone who shrugs and pretends that this thing that drives so much of human behavior, good and bad, somehow just isn't a big deal.

And then, amid your modern doubt that the old religious rules make sense, maybe extend a little bit of the same skepticism to the world that's being made by societies that have tried to simply throw them off. The twenty-first-century developed world, perhaps the most sexually liberated large-scale society in human history, currently suffers from a number of notable social ills: fewer and fewer people are having children, fewer and fewer people are getting married, fewer and fewer people are even having the sex that we supposedly unshackled ourselves from religious dogma in order to enjoy. Meanwhile more people appear to be enslaved to pornography, more people are unhappily celibate, more people are failing to have the number of kids they say they want—if, that is, they have kids at all. The sexes are increasingly alienated from one another, rates of suicide have gone up, there is a surfeit of unhappiness and despair.

Does all of this simply reflect God's just punishment on the human race for abandoning ideals of chastity, or the law of karma coming around to inflict the same punishment impersonally? Surely not: economics and technology and a host of other forces play their own enervating roles. But the social history of the last few decades should, at the very least, disturb one's confidence that the world before the sexual revolution was *simply* oppressive and the world since is *simply* more liberated and just. Instead it should raise the possibility that if the traditional emphasis on chastity and monogamy and marriage— the broadly shared consensus of the world's religions—deserves critique or required some adaptation, if it led to bigotries, cruelties, unjust discrimination, it also may contain important wisdom you can't simply sweep away under the brush of "puritanism" or "patriarchy."

I submit that acknowledging that important possibility, making that concession, is all you need to enter sincerely into the exploration of a traditional religious faith. There is plenty of time to wrestle with the specific questions—Which rules about sex or gender are culturally conditioned? Which are essential to the faith? Should Muslim women wear headscarves? Is the Catholic Church correct to condemn artificial contraception?—as you go deeper into exploration. But the initial obstacle can be surmounted as soon as you stop assuming that any religion with specific rules about sex is necessarily getting everything wrong, and begin to be curious about what that religion's rules might be getting right.

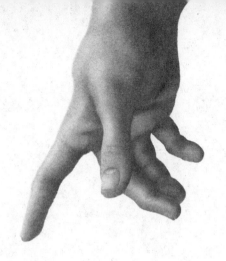

7

# The End of
# Exploring

In the fall of 2023, Ayaan Hirsi Ali, an ex-Muslim critic of Islamic fundamentalism, wrote an essay announcing her conversion to Christianity. Hirsi Ali had grown up in Somalia, where she had been subjected to female genital mutilation and reared under the harsh Wahhabi interpretation of Islam. After moving to the Netherlands in the 1990s to escape a forced marriage, she was converted to Enlightenment liberalism and became part of the circle of the New Atheists, defending secular reason against religious obscurantism and warning against the spread of shari'a law into Europe.

Attacked by both Muslims and left-wing critics of Islamophobia, she gravitated toward the political right and ended up as an American citizen married to the historian Niall Ferguson. By a certain point, she wrote, any sense of liberation for punitive divine authority had faded away, and she found "life without any spiritual solace unendurable." So she groped her way, to her surprise, into a provisional form of Christian faith.[1]

Hirsi Ali's conversion essay attracted a great deal of criticism. Some of it came from betrayed and disappointed atheists, unable to grasp how their brilliant arguments had failed to keep her in the fold. But much of it came from Christians and other religious people, disappointed in the instrumentalist way she talked about her newfound faith. There was little mention of Jesus in her essay, for instance, and a lot of talk about politics and culture war. Hirsi Ali described her growing sense that atheism is too weak a grounding for the Western liberalism that she champions, and that in a world beset by challenges to liberalism, the Christian tradition represents a surer foundation for human dignity and human rights.

Reading the piece, you had the sense that her primary affection was still for the Western world, Europe and the United States, and the political order that had welcomed her. She was seeking spiritual consolation in Christianity more because Christianity was the faith of her beloved West than because she had fallen in love with Jesus Christ Himself.

That was the initial impression, at least, and though her subsequent public comments suggested a greater depth to Hirsi Ali's conversion, let's remain with that impression for a moment—in which someone feeling a need for religion ends up converting to the faith that has the most positive cultural associations, perhaps the faith practiced by some of her friends, the faith that stood readiest to hand whether or not she felt certain of its truth.

In the course of the last two chapters I've tried to simplify the quest for a religious tradition a bit, by separating out what seem like some broad essential questions from the detail and arcana of religious disputation. But I can easily imagine a nonreligious reader feeling like I haven't simplified things enough. *To pick a religious tradition I just have to decide whether I'm polytheist or a classical theist, come to a definite view of damnation versus reincarnation, decide what the problem of evil means for my conception of divinity, and, oh by the way, develop a strong opinion on the historical Jesus, the historical Muhammed, the historical Buddha, and maybe even the historical Krishna as well? Simplicity itself! I'll just quit my job and get right on it!*

There is a snide answer to his complaint, to the effect that many busy secular people manage to find the time to develop incredibly strong views on arcane subjects entirely unrelated to either their daily lives or their eternal destiny. (In our times many a potential theologian has been derailed from his true vocation into a comprehensive study of the Star Wars universe.)

But many modern people are genuinely busy, harried, exhausted. Many people aren't naturally interested even in the more general sort of theological debates. Many people are interested but can see multiple sides to complex questions and aren't likely to resolve on a simple answer to a question like "Should I be a polytheist?" let alone find that answer a sufficient spur to practicing Hinduism.

For those people, I want to offer a permission slip to be a little bit less intense, to leave even some of the big-picture theological questions unresolved, and simply let down your spiritual bucket where you are, or where you want to be. This involves putting your trust, once again, in the hope that God and the universe aren't out to get you, and doing what Hirsi Ali's critics accuse her of doing: entering whatever religious tradition seems to have been placed before you, whether through familial inheritance or social connections or political and cultural affinities, and hope that God placed it there for some good reason.

## When Belief Is an Inheritance

This is, of course, what most religious people already do, usually through the first mechanism, family inheritance—embracing the faith of their fathers and mothers as their own rather than striking out into the religious marketplace. There is more conversion and spiritual migration in America than in most societies, but even here both belief and affiliation are highly heritable; as your family believed growing up, you are much more likely to believe yourself. And even people who move around a bit often do so within a larger inherited context. My own family's tour through American Christianity took us to many spiritual way stations in charismatic and evangelical Christianity, but we began as Episcopalians and twelve years later ended up as Roman Catholics, which from the perspective of the sociology of religion looks like a small leap rather than a large one, a partial homecoming after a period of wandering.

This pattern of inheritance is itself often raised as a point against religious arguments. The philosophically minded economist Tyler Cowen, for instance, in an essay explaining his own unbelief, featured the "heritable aspect" of religious belief as a reason for skepticism "about what we think we know about religious truth."[2] Most believers seem too much like "social conformists" to seem trustworthy when they argue for their respective faiths.

This is the nuanced version of the argument; atheist polemics are filled with more severe attacks on the religious indoctrination of the young, the "child abuse" supposedly visited on young people by their religious parents. But as Cowen notes, atheism turns out to be quite heritable as well; people believing the same things as their parents, religious or irreligious, is just a human default. So heritability doesn't make the case for atheism per se, but rather—he says—for a default to skepticism about any belief that's based on imitation of one's parents or one's peers.

The weakness of Cowen's argument is that his point applies to any worldview, not just to religion. Save in very rare periods of radical tumult, conversion happens on the margin, and converts are by definition the exception rather than the norm. Whatever you believe about any issue is conditioned by your upbringing, whether as a professional economist debating fellow economists, as a Democrat arguing with Republicans or vice versa, or for that matter as a citizen of the United States who prefers liberal democracy to authoritarianism. This should generate humility in belief, sympathy for others who have ended up in different places, but not a default to permanent skepticism, because you still have to choose where you stand on important questions.

For instance, the fact that my heritage conditions me to hold certain beliefs about the sacredness of human life doesn't mean that I should just retreat to agnosticism about whether murder is really wicked, torture is truly terrible, or genocide is actually abominable. I am being a moral conformist when I condemn Adolf Hitler, but that doesn't automatically invalidate the condemnation.

Likewise, the fact that Cowen came of age in the libertarian-leaning Reagan era and teaches at a university that employs a lot of free-market economists doesn't discredit his arguments for libertarianism. He is, like almost all of us, a conformist in some sense, but he still has every right and indeed every obligation to defend the ideas that he believes are true.

Religion, as I have tried to argue throughout these pages, is not some special realm entirely removed from the usual forms of intellectual analysis and debate. Rather it is a realm like others in human affairs, filled with difficult questions that are nonetheless subject to rational analysis, in which there is an obligation to choose a perspective even with the knowledge that this perspective is limited, fallible, and conditioned by one's upbringing and one's environment.

Except, as I have also tried to argue, we have more of an obligation to make a religious choice or a commitment of some kind, given that the potential stakes so far exceed the stakes of association with a political ideology or academic school of thought. In that sense defaulting to a faith that's culturally given, a particular church that feels familiar and comfortable, need not be a failure of spiritual exploration or an abandonment of theological analysis. It can be simply a good start.

Suppose that you were raised United Methodist, and you return to the church of your youth without having decided firmly to believe in Methodist theology (you may not, like some Methodists of my acquaintance, be certain of what that theology even is). You begin by going to church Christmas and Easter and a few other occasions, and work your way up to regular practice—worship, prayer, solidarity, charitable works.

Now suppose that, in fact, the truest religion in the world is not Protestant Christianity but Sunni Islam. Obviously the optimal scenario for you would have been to discover this fact and become a Muslim. But in your hectic American life the likelihood of that discovery was very low; nothing about your (presumably brief) encounters with Islam sparked anything intellectually or spiritually, nothing about your personal context impelled you toward the religion of Muhammed. So are you worse off, in your relationship to Islam's great truth, as a practicing Christian than a religiously homeless agnostic?

Surely not. As a Methodist you are arguably worshiping the

same God as an observant Muslim, through the mediation of a figure, Jesus, who is revered in Islam as a great prophet, relying on scriptures that Muslims consider an anticipation of the greatest Prophet, following a moral code that has a great deal in common with Islamic morality, and expecting a second coming that mirrors the hope many Muslims place in the coming of the messianic Mahdi. They have true belief, but you have at least true-ish belief; you have taken a large step toward the fullness of truth, even if you aren't all the way to where you ought to be.

Now suppose that not Islam but Buddhism, a different and more distant faith, is actually the truest path. As a Methodist you have less in common with an observant Buddhist than you do with a pious Muslim—but still more in common, most likely, than you would if you practiced no faith at all.

In your Protestant church you will not be taught the entire Buddhist truth about the illusions of existence, you will be encouraged to seek the fulfillment of some desires rather than their total abolition, you will be following the merely saintly Christ rather than the perfect or near-perfect Buddha, and you will be blind to the near inevitability of reincarnation and the reality of some of the secondary gods that popular Buddhism worships.

But if you follow the ethics of the Ten Commandments and the Sermon on the Mount you will not be that far off from the Noble Eightfold Path. If you follow Christian practices of prayer, you will be at least tiptoeing toward forms of meditation. Your ideas about the Trinity and the communion of saints will have some incomplete resemblance to Mahayana ideas about the Buddha's three bodies and the role of saintly bodhisattvas in the path to enlightenment. In awaiting Christ's second coming you will arguably have similar expectations to those Buddhists who expect a messianic figure, the Maitreya, to appear at the end of this age and usher in an era of harmony and peace. And if you embrace the self-abnegation inherent in Christianity, the idea of dying to yourself so that you can live in

Christ, you will be at least on the way toward the Buddhist form of enlightenment—and more likely, at the very least, to achieve a beneficial reincarnation, an upward lift rather than an infernal plunge.

Is it better, in these scenarios, to perform the much more thorough investigation of religious alternatives, one that might lead you to recognize the fuller truth in Islam and Buddhism and leave your childhood Methodism behind? Yes, of course, it would be better, much as sainthood is always better than a merely plodding attempt, with a lot of backsliding, to follow the minimum of the moral law. But the gulf between the deep, comprehensive, intense attempt to reach the truth about human existence and the plodding attempt to just get a little bit closer is still much smaller than the gulf between the limited attempt and no attempt at all.

Here the parable of the talents in Matthew's gospel seems like a relevant text. Jesus describes a master who, departing on a journey, leaves one talent (a sum of silver) with one of his servants, two talents with another, and five talents with a third. The one who received five talents and the one who received two talents both invest their gifts, and the first ends up with ten talents, the second with four. But the servant given just one talent, out of fear that his master will be angry if he risks and loses anything, simply buries the talent in the ground. The master returns, and each of the two investors are praised equally, even though one ended up with much more silver, while the servant who fearfully buried his treasure is condemned. "For to everyone who has will more be given, and he will have an abundance. But from the one who has not, even what he has will be taken away."[3]

Another hard saying! But one that should also be comforting, implying as it does that everyone receives different gifts, different opportunities, and you will not be penalized for failing to reach the same exact destination as your neighbor in the course of your spiritual or moral journey. The punishment is reserved for refusing to choose or act, period, for believing in a God or universe that will punish you for taking any steps at all.

So if the only place that seems available to commit your talents is your childhood faith tradition, you should feel no embarrassment at being a conformist or a slavish imitator of your ancestors. God can do infinitely more with imitation than with no activity at all.

## When You Can't Just Return Home

This advice doesn't apply, indeed it's useless or perverse, if your experience with your ancestral faith was miserable or punishing or abusive, as it was for Ayaan Hirsi Ali. Sometimes there's no default, no place of original affiliation and affection, and an attempted return will be impossible or self-destructive. Sometimes you have to purge yourself of an ungodly religious experience before you can begin anything again. For some people, perhaps, that purgation is itself the admirable spiritual effort, the investment of the talents, the movement that carries them toward alignment with the truth. Where religion perpetrates sustained abuse, any truth value it offers usually turns negative, meaning that the cult survivor who escapes and turns agnostic is closer to the truth about the world than the cult adherent who remains loyal to the Kool-Aid's very dregs.

But if you can come through that kind of experience, as Hirsi Ali did—or if, as is true for the increasing number of people who inherited their parents' atheism, you have no religious background or spiritual default at all—then you should still be ready when an open door presents itself, even if you aren't as certain as some converts that you're running toward the fullest truth.

And just as you shouldn't feel shame about returning to your parents' faith, you also shouldn't feel embarrassed to convert for what seem, to the zealous, like insufficient reasons. Because it's the faith of your spouse or children. Because it's the church of your most attractive or inspiring group of friends. Because you feel a special attraction to the civilization that sprang from this particular faith's ideas. Because your favorite novelist is a devout Catholic or a serious Calvinist or an observant Jew. Because some set of strange synchronicities serves to make Buddhism unexpectedly available and attractive. Because you have a brush with radical goodness, even sanctity, that's attached to a specific community or faith.

Given the strictest scrunity, almost every conversion can look impure or incomplete, a matter of mixed motives and personal contingencies. But as long as you aren't throwing yourself headlong into a cult or engaging in some sort of elaborate self-deception, there are few truly bad reasons for abandoning agnosticism in favor of commitment. If your attraction is sincere, if it seems meant to be, if you're out there looking and it feels like what you were supposed to find, then you're better off crossing the threshold and seeing what's inside.

Because you never know where it might go. Some people's encounters with religion in childhood aren't negative or abusive so much as they are just sterile and empty, making the faith of their ancestors feel like a dead letter when it comes time to start on their own journey. That was how it was for the British novelist Paul Kingsnorth. He was raised to experience his isle's Christianity as a hopeless antiquarianism, a thing that mattered only as a foil for modernity. His own adult spiritual progress grew naturally out of his environmentalism, which led him first into a kind of "pick'n'mix spirituality," and then into a commitment to Zen Buddhism, which lasted years but felt insufficient, lacking (he felt) a mode of true worship.[4]

He found that worship in actual paganism, a nature-worship that made sense as an expression of his love of the natural world, and he went so far as to become a priest of Wicca, a practitioner of what he took to be white magic. At which point, and only at that point, he began to feel impelled toward Christianity—by coincidence and dreams, by ideas and arguments, and by the kind of stark mystical experiences discussed in an earlier chapter of this book.

But it would have been unimaginable to him at the start of the journey that the Christian faith imparted weakly in his childhood—that "ancient, tired religion" as he puts it—could have possibly been his destination in the end. No such recognition could have been made on the basis of the initial limp encounter alone. Only the act of questing, of following spiritual threads as he followed other threads throughout his life, could have possibly delivered back to the initial place, no longer old and tired but somehow fresh and new.

"We shall not cease from exploration," wrote T. S. Eliot in his *Four Quartets*, "And the end of all our exploring / Will be to arrive where we started / And know the place for the first time."[5] That's a perfect encapsulation for Kingsnorth's journey in particular. But for the general obligation imposed upon us all, no matter where we start and wherever we might hope to reach, a different Eliot line is apt: "For us, there is only the trying. The rest is not our business."[6]

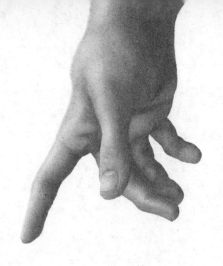

8

# A Case Study:
# Why I Am a Christian

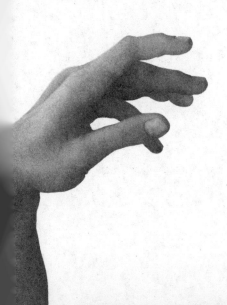

Let's end this long argument with a personal example: my own. I am a Christian, a practicing member of the Roman Catholic Church, a conservative Catholic by the world's standards, a bit more uncertain about my conservative Catholicism than some of my coreligionists, a bit weirder in some of my ideas about the cosmos compared to most of my secular friends and some of my religious ones as well. Have I followed my own advice in coming to my specific religious commitments? You can be the judge.

I'll start with the biography. I was born to upper-middle class Protestant parents and baptized Episcopalian in Connecticut in the 1980s, which means that according to sociological generalization I should have grown up as a Christmas-and-Easter Christian, drifted from religion as an adult, and raised thoroughly secularized children who then went on to explore some form of exotic hallucinogen-mediated spirituality in college.

Instead, my family was diverted by illness and unexpected religious awakening into charismatic Christianity. That's the bland way of saying that I grew up watching crowds of otherwise normal Connecticut Yankees, a population not known for revivalism these days, experience the range of spiritual experiences discussed earlier in this book, from tongues-speaking to supernatural healings to intense, flat-on-the-floor mystical blasts like the one my mother's essay attempted to describe. The openness to the numinous and supernatural that I've urged on secular readers in these pages was, in one sense, organic to my childhood. I couldn't not be open to strange spiritual possibilities because they were being made manifest around me.

But at the same time they weren't my own spiritual encounters. I was an observer, an accidental pilgrim, a passenger carried along by forces I didn't experience myself. The secular adult friends that my parents invited to charismatic services might pitch over and shake mysteriously and rise befuddled by the experience, but under all forms of charismatic prayer I remained unravished and unmoved.

I suppose my impassibility could have set me up for a life of skepticism. But instead I came away quite confident in the reality of what had been happening around me. Confident, that is, that it was emphatically not just a trick of mentalist persuasion, a madness of crowds, or whatever other reductive explanation you might seek—that it was much more real and much more flagrantly supernatural than dry references to "religious experience" in secular publications would lead one to expect.

But because I wasn't personally caught up in it, I had no choice but to approach it analytically rather than mystically, to stand a bit outside it, to play the professor of religious studies even as a twelve-year-old.

The direct experience, for my parents and many others, created a relational religious attitude, a sense of God as a person with whom you could commune. The indirect experience inspired a desire for a system, a theory of the case, a world-picture that made sense of all these strange encounters—which the frame of Official Knowledge offered by my secular education emphatically did not.

## What I Found in Catholic Christianity

All of this made it somewhat predictable that I would end up Roman Catholic, joining the part of Christianity known for systematizing everything, for being dedicated to the proposition that faith and reason are friends rather than rivals and that it's possible to reason about the supernatural and come to plausible conclusions.

But if Catholicism answered my desire for systemization, it also fit my personality in other ways. After standing unmoved so often under charismatic prayer, I especially appreciated Catholicism's sacramental promises, in which the Holy Spirit is assumed to be operational in baptism and confirmation and confession even if you aren't overcome with ecstasy in the moment itself.

The Catholic Church accepts, in other words, that some people have mystical temperaments and some people don't, and it promises that God loves even the nonmystical personality, the impermeable-seeming soul. But it makes this promise without seeming to exclude or limit the mystical. In Catholicism the sheer weirdness of what I saw growing up in charismatic Christianity isn't denied or anathematized. Rather it's matched, exceeded, and enfolded into orthodoxy in the stories of the church's wilder miracles, its stranger saints.

Then, too, I found in Catholicism coherent responses to some of the questions discussed in chapter 5, answers that seemed sensible, balanced, intuitively plausible. The church is a liturgical institution that leaves room for both ethical and radically mystical approaches to religion. It's monotheistic rather than polytheistic but with an understanding of divinity that builds in crucial bridges between the Absolute and the timebound world. Its vision of purgatory as a possible destination for a great many human souls seems like a reasonable balance in the debate over eternal damnation versus reincarnation and universal salvation. And its pluralist cosmology, in which angels and demons and saints exist as spiritual powers in their own right and even the singular Godhead has a mysterious triune relationship within Itself, likewise leavens the philosophical case for a single transcendent Creator with a recognition of the way that spiritual exploration seems to bring people into contact with a range of supernatural beings.

Meanwhile the capaciousness of Catholicism, its antiquity and resilience and global sprawl, makes an obvious fit with my baseline assumption that God isn't just hiding from us, that the big and important religions are big and important for a reason, and that even if they aren't in possession of every iota of the truth they are the safest harbors for the honest seeker. Especially since the big and important religions also tend to harbor real diversity, which has its own advantages to the religious searcher—offering a sense that one can join a faith without settling every spiritual question immediately and that one can change important views without departing. All of which can help sustain both belief and practice across a lifetime—as you change politically, as your circumstances and relationships are altered, as your experience of liturgy or community evolves, as God sends graces or tribulations (or both of them at once).

Of course with global sprawl and influence and intense internal factionalism come a lot of worldliness, a taste for power, and an authoritarian temptation. So I can understand why the entanglements that Catholicism has accumulated, the long history of corruptions, make it hard for many people to believe in the church as a divinely founded institution. Certainly twenty-five years of sex-abuse revelations have given me a much clearer sense of the church's institutional failings that I had when I converted.

But perhaps foolishly my own impulse still runs in the opposite direction. The sins of Catholicism seem inseparable from its sheer significance in history, its in-the-arena influence on civilizations past and yet unborn, its shaping role today on how millions or even billions of people encounter God. Come what may, the Catholic Church seems like an instrument of Providence; come what may it does not seem like it can ever be a bad place for a believer to be planted.

And then finally, in becoming Catholic after a childhood spent in mainline and charismatic Protestantism, I also followed the advice dispensed in the prior chapter—on the one hand, not feeling embarrassed to remain with my childhood faith, my inherited commitments, but also moving to an expression of that faith that resonated more with my own ideas and experiences and personality.

That personality is still as it was in childhood to some degree. I have not become an intense mystic or great spiritual experiencer with age. But I have found in my practice of Catholicism sufficient intimations of the supernatural—nothing radical enough to persuade a skeptic, but notable enough for my own already-believing purposes—to make me feel that I am at least not going wildly wrong.

In the end, any sincere religious quest has to take certain initial experiences and later directional nudges as important givens, letting itself be shaped by the larger shape of life, and not simply refusing the guidance provided by the years that God has granted us to live. I've had a wide range of encounters with religion in my forty-five years. I've read and argued and considered a lot of different currents and ideas, and I don't think I've had any special guidance leading anywhere except Christianity in general, Catholic Christianity in particular.

So in that sense it would be both reckless and ungrateful for me to go anywhere except where I've ended up.

## The Perennialist Possibility

But isn't all this talking around an essential question, which is whether I think the tradition I've ended up practicing is actually true? Not just true enough, not just pointing toward God, not just generally accurate in its description of the nature of God or the cosmos, but true in its most important claims about reality? After all, Catholics don't just stand up on Sundays and proclaim their belief in mono-theism, a diversity of supernatural beings, sacramental grace, and the goodness of creation. We profess belief in "one Lord Jesus Christ, the Only Begotten Son of God, born of the Father before all ages," who came to earth and "by the Holy Spirit was incarnate of the Virgin Mary," who died on the cross in Roman Palestine and "rose again on the third day in accordance with the scriptures," who will eventually "come again in glory to judge the living and the dead." And that is just the creedal condensation of a long list of specific claims about the way to salvation, the requirements of the moral law, the authority of the bishops and the pope—enough to fill a thick-bound catechism, at the very least.

Throughout this book I have stressed an empirical approach to religion, an argument that the raw data of existence implies religious obligations and matches up to religious assumptions. So it's natural to ask if the specific claims of my Catholic Christianity match up in the same way, if the doctrines fit the fact patterns as I've described them and the way of reasoning about religion I've proposed.

Since this isn't a work of Catholic polemic, I'm not going to go through those doctrines one by one and defend each one's fittedness to reality. Instead let me raise what I think is the strongest empirical challenge to the specificity of my beliefs, and then explain why that challenge doesn't overcome my faith.

I've gestured at this challenge already, and it isn't particular to Catholicism, except insofar as Catholicism is itself extremely particular in its claims. It's the tension between the evidence we have regarding spiritual experience and the specificity of any single faith tradition.

If we assume, as this book does, that religious experience is a crucial source of religious belief, if we take the mystical and supernatural and miraculous seriously in a comprehensive way, what we find are broad patterns that point toward a general architecture of the universe. But we also find a real diversity, in both positive and negative experiences but especially the positive ones, that seems personally and culturally mediated rather than vindicating a universal vision of the truth.

To be clear, I think there are many visions and miracles and compelling mystical experiences that speak to the credibility of Christianity. Further, there are some specific arenas where I could make a case that Christianity generally and Catholicism especially seem to exert unusual power, relative to other spiritual traditions, over certain inhuman-seeming forces. (Yes, I'm talking about demonology and the occult: reading deeply about possession and exorcism, or talking to people involved in the more intense cases, is one of the best ways to inspire yourself to get to Sunday Mass every week.)

But I do not have a complex regression analysis to prove that

Christianity gets you more miracles, more healings, more super-natural encounters than all its major rivals. And even if I did, some supernatural experiences are clearly human universals, not just the special province of any single faith, and both the prosaic and out-rageous encounters with the divine that show up throughout Catholic history have some analogs in other major faiths.

It's also clearly the case that the kinds of mystical experiences that people expect somehow shape the experiences they have. As noted previously, there are more reports of past lives being recalled in countries with a strong belief in reincarnation, more encounters with Krishna in India and Jesus in Indiana, more encounters with ghosts in cultures that believe strongly in ancestral spirits (as in Japan after the tsunami), and so on. And then there are various encounters, like what we see with the UFO phenomenon, that don't necessarily fit with any theology at all.

As I've already argued, the existence of the weird supernatural isn't per se a problem for Christian belief, nor is a diversity in the kinds of spiritual experiences that different cultures condition people to go looking for (and sometimes find). Christians can believe in ghosts so long as we don't become too fascinated by them, we can believe in fairies or their equivalents (as the medievals did) as well as angels and demons, we can believe that there are all sorts of strange things going on around us that God in His wisdom hasn't seen fit to clarify or reveal, and we can even believe that there are God-ordained exceptions (an occasional reincarnation, who can say?) to the rules He *has* revealed to us.

But overall, if you just look at the general evidence from super-natural experience, you might conclude that Christianity is one particular potent expression of the truth, one particularly powerful interpretation of the raw material of religious experience—but not necessarily that it has an exclusive claim to be the one true faith.

Take an example like near-death experiences: Many recurrent features are compatible with Christian doctrine—some kind of life review or judgment, some kind of divine encounter, a sense of heavenly welcome in many cases, a purgatorial or hellish experience in others. But it's still the case that everyone who comes back from the threshold of death doesn't report meeting Jesus (or Mary or Saint Peter), that the Hindu is more likely to see gods where the Christian sees angels, and there is both a culture-bound diversity and a deep mystery to the reports rather than a simple confirmation of the Christian schematic of heaven and hell, death and judgment.

Which, indeed, is why some Christian writers on the subject—the Orthodox monk Seraphim Rose, for instance—have warned that these experiences actually constitute a deception, a demonic attempt to make people returned to life feel assured of their salvation or to instill a belief in universalism against the claims of Christian orthodoxy.[1]

I do think specific spiritual snares exist, but as ever I am skeptical that God would allow pervasive deception of the kind that would have to be involved if all non-Christian mystical encounters were traps or misdirections. Instead, I think the orthodox Christian (or any believer in the specific truth of a particular religion) has to assume both that the divine meets us where we are, even using the imagery and symbolism of other faiths, and also that there is a little more mystery to the supernatural realm than even a theological system founded on divine revelation can completely capture.

But from these concessions it's only a little distance to a perspective like "perennialism," which is the idea that the permanent truths about God and the cosmos are encoded in different forms in different great religions, such that it makes sense to approach divinity through any of them, but not to imagine that any single tradition has sole access to the most important truth.

Since my argument throughout this book sometimes veers close to this point of view—in my emphasis on the convergence between great religions, say—and the broad evidence of mystical experience seems to point in a perennialist direction, why not just conclude that this theory probably has things right?

I could still practice Christianity inside this framework; indeed, I could still practice a quite conservative form of Christianity, on the theory that this is the religious map that God has given me for my own life, and that one should try to follow a specific map as closely as possible rather than assuming that you can just layer different charts atop each other and reach the same destination.

I could be a dogmatist, in other words, in prayer and deed and moral vision, on the grounds that Catholic Christianity should be true to itself, true to its share of God's larger revelation—all the while remaining a bit more agnostic about how much of the full religious picture is captured by the Nicene Creed. I could maintain what the Jesuits call "mental reservation" when I say it—endorsing, but also holding back; standing with the faith that God has given me, but also a little bit apart.

## The Strangest Story in the World

But when I say the Nicene Creed, I mean it. I am open to hidden complexities and unexpected syntheses, but in the end I think that God has acted in history through Jesus of Nazareth in a way that differs from every other tradition and experience and revelation, and the Gospels should therefore exert a kind of general interpretative control over how we read all the other religious data. This is my answer to chapter 5's final and most important question: I think the New Testament is just clearly *different* from other religious texts in a way that stands out and demands attention, that the figure of Jesus likewise stands out among religious founders, that together the sources and the story and the Nazarene Himself all seem God-touched to a degree unmatched by any of their rivals. So where there is uncertainty, tension, a wager to be made, I make my bet on Jesus.

My reasons return us to where we began in the first chapter, to all the supposed victories of skepticism over religion that are not, in fact, such triumphant victories after all. One of those alleged victories was the triumph of historical-critical scholarship over the credibility of the Bible in general and the Christian Gospels in particular. Its great project, deconstructing the New Testament to discover a "historical Jesus" distinct from the Christ of faith, has convinced a great many people that there's little that's fully trustworthy in Matthew, Mark, Luke, and John. Instead they're offering a mixture of mythmaking and confabulation, composed long after the fact to suit disparate political or theological agendas or cover up inconvenient aspects of the real story—that Jesus was a political revolutionary or an apolitical sage, that He had a wife or a Roman-centurion father, that He never said most of the things attributed to Him, that He never even existed.

But this skeptical conviction is founded on sand. Approach the strongest evidence about early Christianity without preconceptions, and you will discover that just as modern science has raised questions for particular theologies, modern scholarship has raised questions for particular interpretations of the New Testament. (For instance, by identifying or amplifying various tensions between the four gospels, undermining the schools of biblical inerrancy that hold that no sacred author could possibly make a mistake about chronology or report a parable inexactly.) But when it comes to the basic historicity of the gospel narratives, their proximity to the events described, their claim to be eyewitness accounts, their credibility relative to the various "lost gospels" that were left out of the canon, it is the revisionists to the revisionists—the scholars deconstructing deconstructionism— who have far and away the better of the argument.

I recommend reading deeply in these academic arguments if you're interested, from Richard Bauckham's *Jesus and the Eyewitnesses* and the heavy tomes of the Anglican bishop and scholar N. T. Wright to shorter works like Peter J. Williams' pellucid *Can We Trust the Gospels?*[2] But to summarize, the case is simple enough. The four gospels have no credible rivals when it comes to their historical proximity to the events of Jesus' life. The vast corpus of extracanonical gospels that attracted so much twentieth-century interest tells us a lot about later arguments in Christianity but next to nothing about its origins, whereas the four gospels all date plausibly to the earliest generations of the church. The Gospels display a deep familiarity with the landscape and culture of their setting: the local geography and topography, the names of minor towns as well as cities, the descriptions of certain features that archaeology has only recently discovered, the names that would have been popular at that time and place, and more. They display a consistent pattern of what Lydia McGrew dubs "undesigned coincidences,"[3] in which passing references and stray details in one gospel will fit neatly into holes left or questions raised in another gospel's narrative, and read together their narratives often help make sense of one another—not only the three synoptic gospels, with their clear overlap, but the gospel of John as well.[4] Strip away the supernatural claims, or the secular bias against accounts that include such claims, and the Gospels would be treated as remarkably credible historical sources—more credible than what we have available for many notable figures in the ancient world, and certainly more credible than the sources for the origin of many other faiths.

And credible even in their traditional claims to represent the memories of the actual disciples and early followers of Christ—with Mark supposedly transcribing Peter's recollections, Luke collecting testimony from the multiple sources that he mentions at the outset of his gospel, Matthew's nativity story seeming to originate with Joseph and Luke's nativity with Mary, and John carrying a specific set of memories of Jesus' most intimate words to the disciples. These attributions have been dismissed by the various historical-Jesus projects, but they tend to return as those projects dissolve, because people notice once again all the memoiristic details that match up with the traditionally imputed authorship.[5]

From the gospel of Mark, with its memorable Aramaic flourishes ("*epthaha*," Jesus says as He heals the blind man) that make sense if a

Galilean fisherman was his crucial source, to the distinctive perspective on the passion and crucifixion in John that makes sense as the vantage point of the one disciple who didn't flee after Gethsemane—if these are not eyewitness accounts, they are remarkable simulations of the same. You have to approach the gospels with a skeptic's zeal or a lawyerly defensiveness not to be struck by their memoiristic qualities—their immediacy and intimacy, the unsanded roughness of their portrayals of Jesus and His inner circle, the mix of personal intensity and theological uncertainty that informs their storytelling. The gospel writers are sure that they're telling the most important story in the world, but with the exception of the theologically minded author of John's gospel they don't even try to sell you definitively on what it's all supposed to mean; like a contemporary memoirist they seem to still be processing the events themselves. As C. S. Lewis puts it, it's possible to believe that they're all doing some kind of brilliantly successful impersonation of an eyewitness narration. But someone who tells you that they read like propaganda penned long after the fact "has simply not learned to read."[6]

Indeed, some of the small discrepancies invoked by skeptics to prove that the New Testament isn't perfectly inerrant are part of what confirms this memoiristic impression. The variations in which day a particular event took place, who was present for a given miracle, which exact words someone used, are precisely what you'd expect from a collection of authentic testimonies that weren't smoothed out into propaganda. Likewise for all the difficult sayings and ambiguous teachings that Christians and skeptics have been wrangling over ever since. There is no sense that any of the Gospels are written with a definite theology "pre-baked," as it were, with everything inconvenient retconned or written out. Instead you get the tensions between, say, John's theological emphasis on Christ's divinity and his narrative portrayal of a very human Jesus—seemingly annoyed by His mother at the wedding at Cana, or weeping outside Lazarus's tomb. This certainly extends to the passion and the resurrection narratives; indeed, the mystification of the writers is nowhere more apparent than in those befuddled passages, where the disciples first abandon their Master and despair of their cause, then misunderstand and fail to recognize the miracle, while struggling to consistently portray a resurrected Messiah who comes to them one moment as a superbeing passing through walls and the next as a friend on the seashore eating fish.

You don't have to accept their miraculous claims to recognize that these are all very strange texts indeed. And not just by secular standards; also by the standards of rival religious traditions and the general run of spiritual experiences that this book has already discussed.

For instance, the virgin birth and the resurrection resemble various myths and legends in non-Christian traditions, a fact beloved of skeptics and deconstructers—but conspicuously without the veil of "long ago" or "once upon a time" or the protective haze of prehistory. Instead the events are all reported in the light of recorded chronology, in the midst of a powerful civilization at its peak, with specific witnesses called and referenced, specific places and events and political figures constantly invoked, a running claim to historical grounding that has held up well against endless critical examinations. If it is mythmaking, it's a very unusual kind—a myth that wants to deny that it's a myth and persuade you that it's something entirely different than the dying-god stories in Norse or Greek or Aztec mythology, and manages to achieve remarkable historical verisimilitude even if it leaves you unconvinced.

Or again, Jesus appears as a preacher, an itinerant sage, a prophetic holy man in ways that show continuity with other figures in religious literature and history. But the Gospels are insistent that what matters most isn't His moral or ethical wisdom or His wise detachment from the pains and pleasures of the flesh, but rather His bloody, agonized, abandoned-by-God death at the hands of the great religious and political powers of the world. The suffering isn't the thing to be transcended, somehow, but the very point: the sage does not dwell on the mountaintop or in the wilderness, attracting acolytes and imitators, but descends into Jerusalem, into the maelstrom of history, to meet His fate. And in that descent He doesn't manifest the kind of detachment from the world that unites figures as various as Socrates and the Buddha. No, He's destroyed, crushed, weeping tears of blood in the garden of Gethsemane and crying against God's abandonment on the cross—before rising transfigured, still bearing His wounds.

That transfiguration, too, is a peculiar case. Many religious traditions, from Old Testament Judaism to Eastern Orthodoxy to Tibetan Buddhism, portray particularly holy men and women very occasionally passing through some kind of bodily transformation, either following a specific divine encounter or upon the attainment of some form of near-perfection or enlightenment. Indeed, there is an account like that in the New Testament itself, the transfiguration on Mount Tabor, when Jesus appears in a radiant and glorified form to a few of His disciples (who are as confused as ever, of course) alongside Moses and Elijah.

But that moment isn't the culmination of the story. Jesus' flesh isn't glorified at the end of a holy or exemplary life, with His body then taken up to heaven like Elijah or Enoch in the Old Testament or the Virgin Mary in Catholic tradition. Nor is His flesh transmuted into a mysterious "rainbow body," as in some striking accounts of dying Buddhist sages who seem to evanesce.[7] Instead the glorification on Mount Tabor is a prelude to total desolation, in which Jesus conspicuously isn't taken up by God, doesn't transmute Himself or disappear, but instead is subjected to beatings, scourging, torture, and the most cruel sort of execution. Then and only then does the full transfiguration and subsequent ascension take place: not as the endpoint of a saintly or holy life but as an unexpected second act, all-but-unprecedented in the annals of prophets and mystical personalities.

That second act, in turn, has unprecedented religious consequences. Like other figures in religious history Jesus is a founder
who promises His followers a great kingdom, a Messiah who claims
a special relationship with God. But unlike Moses or Muhammed (or
for that matter the founders of most American religious movements,
from Mormonism to Christian Science to Scientology) He founds and
forges nothing concrete and visible in His earthly lifetime, delivering
neither a new political order, nor a new religious structure, nor a new
sacred scripture to His followers. Instead all the writing and all the
building is done by others in His name, without benefit of political
power or other forms of worldly recompense, often under threat of
martyrdom, for decades and centuries after the events at Calvary.
Certainly the builders claim to be following Christ's dictates and
example, spreading the gospel as He commanded them. But their
work is done after His departure, in obedience to a shared experience,
in a decentralized way that carries on without a single charismatic
leader (notwithstanding the special importance of Paul, Peter, and
others) for hundreds of years before it finally becomes intertwined
with political power.

And when earthly power finally comes to Christianity, it isn't
just the power of one cult replacing another. The triumph of the
Christian message instantiates a profound revolution in the moral and
spiritual order of the world, one so profound that two thousand years
later it's still taken for granted, treated as bedrock, by many people
who imagine themselves to have left Christianity behind.

The revolution's core idea—that suffering can be nobler than
strength, that the meek and poor might inherit the earth, that God
is on the side of the struggling and sick against the powerful and
strong—can be found elsewhere in the great religions of the world;
it's part of the general religious convergence described earlier in this
book. But with Christianity the idea moves very suddenly from the
prophetic margins to the very center of Roman civilization. With
Christianity the cross, the symbol of tortured human suffering, is

elevated above the world's iconography of strength and beauty, of Apollo or Hercules or Aphrodite. With Christianity we are told that God Himself is on that cross, and through the cross He is with us also, in all our suffering and to the end of time. And with that movement comes one possible answer to some of the hardest questions people have about God's distance, God's silence, the problem of evil and the problem of sin—not in the form of a logical proof but as a story, an event, a person who also happened to be God.

As the British historian Tom Holland puts it in *Dominion*, his survey of Christianity's astonishing rise, it is the counterintuitive boldness on display here, the audacity "of finding in a twisted and defeated corpse the glory of the creator of the universe," that explains "the sheer strangeness of Christianity, and of the civilization to which it gave birth."[8]

## God's Fingerprints in History

What is all of this strangeness supposed to prove? Well, at the very least, that the origin of Christianity looms as a supreme feat of human religious creativity, a bold leap in morality and philosophy and aesthetics that would have seemed absurd or very strange if you'd described its specific claims beforehand. The fact that this supreme leap was achieved by a motley band of Jewish provincials—not uneducated provincials, that's an understatement, but clearly not at all the set that you would have focused on if you were charged with studying the important intellectual schools of Augustan or Claudian Rome—also makes it a supreme feat of outsider-driven revolution, distinct from the usual way that ideas develop and circulate inside developed civilizations. The fact that it was achieved after total desolation and defeat for its Messiah, in an hour when by any reasonable worldly standard the Jesus movement should have been completely crushed, makes whatever happened to the disciples in the days after the crucifixion one of the most striking psychological events in the history of movements and ideas.

So to believe that the core claims of Christianity are false, their essential features either mistaken or made up, is to believe that a kind of extraordinary, even divine genius descended on its creators in the least propitious circumstances, delivering to them a mythopoetic narrative that was somehow perfectly designed to transform the Roman world and spread around the globe. This divinely-inspired-genius theory of Christian origins is basically where certain forms of liberal Christianity and Christian-friendly spirituality have ended up—trying to preserve the power of the story, the sense of its divine authorship, while divesting themselves from the claims about a body rising from the tomb. The idea might be that sometimes God or the Universe grants specific communities a revelation about the truth of existence that's encoded in a fundamentally legendary story, and that in the case of Jesus of Nazareth the myth's power worked, the deepest truth could be unveiled, only if the people involved believed, honestly but incorrectly, that it had really happened to them.

But if you start with the broad conclusions that this book urges on its readers—that the universe looks both made and made for us, that the human mind seems to have a cosmic purpose, that spiritual and supernatural realities seem to impinge constantly on our own—then you should be willing to go a bit farther and consider the possibility that something even wilder and crazier than just a spiritually fruitful mass delusion happened to the early Christians between Good Friday and Pentecost. If you accept the reality of spiritual happenings and religious events, this looks more like an Event—a huge spike on the graph, a mountain among foothills, not a flash of light but a window flung wide open.

Recall Christopher Hitchens' question for me in the DC kitchen: "If Jesus did rise from the dead, what would that really prove?" The easy answer is that it should at least make someone like Hitchens a lot more interested in the truth claims of religion. But really I think one can go much farther than this, and once again for reasons connected to this book's core assumption that God is not trying to trick us, that if the universe offers us clues to its purpose we should follow them with confidence, that the path to truth may be extremely hard but it shouldn't be deceptive or impossible.

This implies that if you find within human history (not just human myth and legend) a singular and well-attested happening, an especially dramatic and compelling story set in an especially earthy and human context, through which the order of the world was forever altered, a religious event seems to stand out starkly from the historical record; if this event looks stranger and more credibly miraculous than other religious foundings; if the specific nature of its miracle seems to stand out from the wider range of stories about saints and sages and holy men and women; if its sheer strangeness still echoes down the centuries despite all the attempts at reinterpretation and domestication—well, then the simplest interpretation of that discovery is also the literal-minded one: that the resurrection really happened, that here God intervened in human affairs decisively, that this is the defining revelation of His purposes, in whose light the larger run of mystical and spiritual experiences across cultures and civilizations should be read. The reasonable thing to do is not just to pay attention but to believe.

Now, maybe to you the New Testament seems more prosaic or more like propaganda, the origins of Christianity not so different from the origins of any other faith. Maybe some other historical moment or revelation seems more inexplicable, more of a black swan in the annals of belief. In which case, by all means, pick up that thread instead! But this is my own conclusion, reaffirmed every time I return to the Gospels and the history that surrounds them, and every time my church enters into Lent and Holy Week, when the crux of the story comes into special focus once again. It's what keeps me bound to real Christian belief—to Easter and not just spiritual perennialism, to Jesus of Nazareth and not just the "Christian tradition." And bound, as well, to the religion that sprang from this Event, the schools of thought that try to explain it, the institutions that are founded upon it, the creeds established by the early church.

All of these deserve attention, loyalty, and deference not because you can be absolutely certain that Christianity generally or my own Roman Catholicism in particular is getting every single issue right. (Protestants have been arguing about what an authoritative Scripture actually authoritatively teaches for going on five centuries, and papal infallibility comes with innumerable qualifications.) But having gone to all this trouble to overturn the normal operation of the world, to enter His own story as a character rather than an author, it seems unlikely that God would then permit the people responsible for stewarding His most important revelation to quickly get everything—about prayer, about sex, about hell, about any other vexed issue—completely and entirely wrong.

If the cross is really the axis of world history, the most important of all supernatural interventions, then Christians might well err and sin and go astray. But the God of history would be a deceiver, not a loving father, if He allowed the entirety of Christianity to be defined by blunders, blind alleys, and mistakes.

## The Urgency of Jesus

This idea of trust or deference to historic Christianity might be interpreted, by the more self-confident spiritual explorers, as a kind of comfort-seeking impulse—putting your trust in the Nicene Creed or the Holy Bible or Mother Church to avoid shouldering too much existential angst or risk, submitting your own judgment to the sup- posed authority of Christian orthodoxy rather than simply taking responsibility for your own beliefs.

In my own case, though, it's not really about comfort at all. The kind of religion that I might work out entirely for myself—based on my private interpretation of the cosmos, my experience of life and the general data offered by religious experience—would be somewhat more relaxed and reassuring than Catholicism or Christianity in its major historical expressions. As a perennialist with Christian sympathies, the most plausible alternative version of my religious self, I would still be attuned to spiritual dangers and the reality of demonic powers, still something less than a groovy New Age optimist. But my personal, artisanally crafted religion would certainly be more optimistic about the salvation of every human soul, less stark in its condemnations and anathemas, than any traditional form of Christian faith.

And then even those traditions, Catholic and Orthodox and Protestant, can seem more reassuring at times than just the stark words of Jesus by themselves—the brusque warnings about the narrow gate and the needle's eye, the condemned goats and foolish virgins and the wide path to destruction. "But from the one who has not, even what he has will be taken away."[9]

Of course Jesus has many other words as well, words of forgiveness and love and understanding and reconciliation—the prodigal welcomed, the late-arriving laborer rewarded, the light burden and the easy yoke. But I have never found the Son of Man as reassuring a character as some Christians do, or quite achieved the sense of personal relationship that gives so many of my co-believers comfort. Like many Catholics I appreciate the saints for their human relatability, the Virgin Mary for her maternal warmth, the Holy Spirit for its faithful presence. Whereas even in human form, walking the hills of Galilee and feeding the multitude and healing the paralytic, the second person of the Godhead still seems more distant, potent, fearful, mysterious, intense.

This, too, is part of why I believe: because the Jesus of Scripture *isn't* always the Savior that my native self finds relatable, the kind of God I would have invented for myself, because there is a tension between some of His hardest and most inscrutable sayings and my own personality, my natural intellectual perspective, my instincts and desires.

What Jesus brings especially, that cuts against my temperament, is a special sort of urgency—a sense that there are not in fact eons of potentially reincarnated existence or innumerable stages of an afterlife in which to work out our destiny, nor a guarantee that the divine desire to reconcile all things will triumph over our own rebellion no matter how far we go astray.

Maybe it will, but for the time being we are given warning after warning not to let this moment go to waste—because our life could be demanded of us at any moment, because at the hour we least expect the Master could unexpectedly return.

This is where I will end my argument as well, balancing my own spirit of irenic optimism with the intensity of the Gospels. The theme of this book is encouragement: to urge people toward religion generally, to suggest that it's better to start somewhere even if it isn't the place I would start, out of a trust that God's providence will ultimately reward all sorts of efforts and enfold all manner of sincere beliefs. And I do believe this. The difficulty of human life, the burdens that each one of us carries, the mystery inherent even in a cosmos that offers good reasons to believe—all of this makes me optimistic that God will repay even the most mediocre effort, the halting attempt to reach upward to the truth, the good-faith attempt to understand our purposes that doesn't necessarily reach the mark.

But if no one will be condemned who has made that effort, it is therefore all the more urgent that we try. Life is short and death is certain, and what account will you give of yourself if the believers turn out to have been right all along? That you took pointlessness for granted in a world shot through with signs of meaning and design? That you defaulted to unbelief because that seemed like the price of being intellectually serious or culturally respectable? That you were too busy to be curious, too consumed with things you knew to be passing to cast a prayer up to whatever eternity awaits?

"Therefore stay awake—for you do not know when the master of the house will come, in the evening, or at midnight, or when the rooster crows, or in the morning—lest he come suddenly and find you asleep."[10]

If you are this sleeper, I beg of you—awake.

# Notes

## Introduction

1. For a useful discussion of these intellectual trends, see Justin Brierley, *The Surprising Rebirth of Belief in God* (Carol Stream, IL: Tyndale, 2023).
2. Derek Thompson, "The True Cost of the Churchgoing Bust," *Atlantic*, April 3, 2024, www.theatlantic.com/ideas/archive/2024/04 /america-religion-decline-non-affiliated/677951/.
3. Karen Armstrong, *The Case for God* (New York: Knopf, 2009), xiii.
4. Armstrong, *Case for God*, xii.
5. Terry Eagleton, "Lunging, Flailing, Mispunching," *London Review of Books*, October 19, 2006, www.lrb.co.uk/the-paper/v28/n20/terry -eagleton/lunging-flailing-mispunching.

## Chapter 1: The Fashioned Universe

1. Tom Stoppard, *Jumpers* (New York: Grove Press, 1972). I should note my debt to Adam Gopnik's 2014 *New Yorker* essay on belief and atheism for calling the line to my attention: www.newyorker.com /magazine/2014/02/17/bigger-phil.
2. Ps. 19:1.
3. For one recent example of an attempted reconciliation, see Mariusz Tabaczek, *Theistic Evolution: A Contemporary Aristotelian-Thomistic Perspective* (Cambridge: Cambridge University Press,

2023). I do not find any of the proposed reconciliations perfectly satisfactory, but that is a subject for a different book.

4. Steven Weinberg, *Dreams of a Final Theory* (New York: Random House, 1994), 251.

5. Stephen M. Barr, *Modern Physics and Ancient Faith*. The case-study examples of fine-tuning are drawn from chapter 15, but the entire book rewards attention.

6. Stephen Hawking, *A Brief History of Time* (London: Bantam Dell, 2017), 130.

7. Paul Davies, *Cosmic Jackpot* (Boston: Mariner Books, 2007).

8. Fred Hoyle, "The Universe: Past and Present Reflections," *Annual Review of Astronomy and Astrophysics* 20, 1982.

9. For an account of the conversation in which Fermi asked his question, see Eric M. Jones, "Where Is Everybody? An Account of Fermi's Question," Los Alamos National Laboratory, 1985, https://sgp.fas.org/othergov/doe/lanl/la-10311-ms.pdf.

10. Spencer Klavan, "Where Mind Meets Matter," *Claremont Review of Books*, Summer 2023, https://claremontreviewofbooks.com/where-mind-meets-matter/.

11. Elaine Howard Ecklund et al., "Religion among Scientists in International Context: A New Study of Scientists in Eight Regions," *Socius* 2 (2016).

12. Richard Lewontin, "Billions and Billions of Demons," *New York Review of Books*, January 9, 1997, www.nybooks.com/articles/1997/01/09/billions-and-billions-of-demons/.

13. For an especially pungent critique of Krauss, see David Albert, "On the Origin of Everything," *New York Times*, March 23, 2012, www.nytimes.com/2012/03/25/books/review/a-universe-from-nothing-by-lawrence-m-krauss.html.

14. Hawking, *A Brief History of Time*, 190.

15. Stephen Hawking and Leonard Mlonidow, *The Grand Design* (New York: Bantam, 2010). See also Stephen Barr's comments and critique: "Much Ado about 'Nothing': Stephen Hawking and the Self-Creating

Universe," *First Things*, September 2010, www.firstthings.com/web-exclusives/2010/09/much-ado-about-nothing-stephen-hawking-and-the-self-creating-universe.

16. *Srimad Bhagavatam* 6:16:37.

## Chapter 2: The Mind and the Cosmos

1. Tom Wolfe, "Sorry, but Your Soul Just Died," *Forbes*, 1996, www3.nd.edu/~afreddos/courses/43151/WolfeSoulDied.php.htm.

2. Roxanne Khamsi, "Jennifer Aniston Strikes a Nerve," *Nature*, June 22, 2005, www.nature.com/articles/news050620-7.

3. Henry Kissinger, Eric Schmidt, and Daniel Huttenlocher, "ChatGPT Heralds an Intellectual Revolution," *Wall Street Journal*, February 24, 2023, www.wsj.com/articles/chatgpt-heralds-an-intellectual-revolution-enlightenment-artificial-intelligence-homo-technicus-technology-cognition-morality-philosophy-774331c6.

4. Casper Wilstrup, "The Implications of Conscious AI: A Leap into the Unknown," *Medium*, June 5, 2023, https://medium.com/machine-cognition/the-implications-of-conscious-ai-a-leap-into-the-unknown-f666f842aad9.

5. David Chalmers, "Facing Up to the Problem of Consciousness," *Journal of Consciousness Studies* 2, no. 3 (1995): 200–219. See also Chalmers, *The Conscious Mind: In Search of a Fundamental Theory* (Oxford: Oxford University Press, 1996).

6. Erik Hoel, "Neuroscience Is Pre-Paradigmatic. Consciousness Is Why," *Intrinsic Perspective*, January 9, 2024, www.theintrinsicperspective.com/p/neuroscience-is-pre-paradigmatic.

7. Hoel, "Neuroscience."

8. Gottfried Leibniz, *The Monadology*, section 17, www.plato-philosophy.org/wp-content/uploads/2016/07/The-Monadology-1714-by-Gottfried-Wilhelm-LEIBNIZ-1646-1716.pdf.

9. Steven Pinker, *How the Mind Works* (New York: Norton, 2009), 558–59, Kindle.

10. For an entertaining disputation on this question see John Searle and

Daniel Dennett, "'The Mystery of Consciousness': An Exchange," *New York Review of Books*, December 21, 1995, www.nybooks.com /articles/1995/12/21/the-mystery-of-consciousness-an-exchange/.

11. If I seem to be returning rather frequently to the maternal example, it's because my wife is the author of the best book on what we *can* know about the science of the maternal transformation: Abigail Tucker, *Mom Genes: Inside the New Science of Our Ancient Maternal Instinct* (New York: Gallery Books, 2021).

12. David Bentley Hart, *The Experience of God* (New Haven: Yale University Press, 2013), 174–75.

13. Thomas Nagel, *Mind and Cosmos* (Oxford: Oxford University Press, 2012), 55–56.

14. Thomas Nagel, "What Daniel Dennett Gets Wrong," *New Statesman*, October 21, 2023, www.newstatesman.com/the-weekend-essay/2023 /10/philosopher-daniel-dennett.

15. Edward J. Neafsey, "Conscious Intention and Human Action: Review of the Rise and Fall of the Readiness Potential and Libet's Clock," *Consciousness and Cognition* 94 (2021).

16. For a recent argument that follows some of this book's premises to panpsychist conclusions, see Philip Goff, *Galileo's Error: Foundations for a New Science of Consciousness* (New York: Pantheon, 2019).

17. Nagel, *Mind and Cosmos*, 72.

18. For an argument for skepticism about *all* forms of reason and knowledge under materialist conditions, see Alvin Plantinga, "Against Naturalism," in Alvin Plantinga and Mark Tooley, *Knowledge of God* (Oxford: Blackwell, 2008).

19. Nagel, *Mind and Cosmos*, 74.

20. Hart, *Experience of God*, 234.

## Chapter 3: The Myth of Disenchantment

1. Michael Shermer, "Anomalous Events That Can Shake One's Skepticism to the Core," *Scientific American*, October 2014; see also

Shermer, *Heavens on Earth: The Scientific Search for the Afterlife, Immortality, and Utopia* (New York: Henry Holt, 2018), 113–16.

2. Barbara Ehrenreich, *Living with a Wild God* (New York: Grand Central Publishing, 2014), 116.

3. David Hume, *An Inquiry Concerning Human Understanding*, section X: "Of Miracles," www3.nd.edu/~afreddos/courses/43811 /hume-on-miracles.htm.

4. The best recent accounts of the UFO phenomenon as protoreligion can be found in D. W. Pasulka, *American Cosmic: UFOs, Religions, Technology* (Oxford University Press, 2019), and Pasulka, *Encounters: Experiences with Nonhuman Intelligences* (New York: St. Martin's, 2023).

5. Sam Knight, *The Premonitions Bureau* (New York: Penguin Press, 2022).

6. Though my own categorizations are somewhat different I am grateful to the schematic offered in David B. Yaden and Andrew B. Newberg, *The Varieties of Spiritual Experience: Twenty-First-Century Research and Perspectives* (Oxford: Oxford University Press, 2022).

7. R. C. Zaehner, *At Sundry Times: An Essay in the Comparison of Religion* (London: Faber and Faber, 1958), 73.

8. Bertrand Russell, *The Autobiography of Bertrand Russell* (New York: Routledge, 2009), 137.

9. William James, *Varieties of Religious Experience* (1917; Project Gutenberg, 2024), 68, www.gutenberg.org/cache/epub/621/pg621 -images.html.

10. Ehrenreich, *Living with a Wild God*, 116.

11. Patricia Snow, "Grace," *First Things*, January 2019, www.firstthings .com/article/2019/01/grace.

12. Ikechukwu Obialo Azuonye, "Diagnosis Made by Hallucinatory Voices," *British Medical Journal* 315 (December 1997).

13. For an account of exorcism's recent growth, see Mike Mariani, "American Exorcism," *The Atlantic*, December 2018, www.the

atlantic.com/magazine/archive/2018/12/catholic-exorcisms-on-the
-rise/573943/. In general I am hesitant to recommend reading on
issues related to the demonic, but a place to start would be with two
quite different works by practicing psychiatrists: Richard Gallagher,
*Demonic Foes* (New York: HarperCollins, 2020), and M. Scott Peck,
*People of the Lie* (New York: Touchstone, 1983).

14. Deborah Blum, *Ghost Hunters: William James and the Search for Scientific Proof of Life after Death* (New York: Penguin Press, 2006), 125–26.

15. Matt. 7:7.

16. T. M. Luhrmann, "When Things Happen That You Can't Explain," *New York Times*, March 5, 2015. www.nytimes.com/2015/03/05 /opinion/when-things-happen-that-you-cant-explain.html.

17. Carlos Eire, *They Flew* (New Haven: Yale University Press, 2023).

18. Craig Keener, *Miracles: The Credibility of the New Testament Accounts* (Grand Rapids: Baker Academic, 2011), 204–5.

19. Keener, *Miracles*, esp. part 3: "Miracle Accounts beyond Antiquity."

20. The best work on saint-making in the Catholic Church remains Kenneth Woodward, *Making Saints* (New York: Simon and Schuster, 1991).

21. Clarissa Romez et al., "Case Report of Gastroparesis Healing: Sixteen Years of a Chronic Syndrome Resolved after Proximal Intercessory Prayer," *Complementary Therapies in Medicine* 43 (2019): 289–94.

22. For true love, see "Most Americans Claim to Have Experienced True Love," CBS News, February 13, 2022, www.cbsnews.com/news /americans-experience-true-love-opinion-poll-02-2022/. For mystical experiences, see Russell Heimlich, "Mystical Experiences," Pew Research Center, December 29, 2009, www.pewresearch.org/short -reads/2009/12/29/mystical-experiences/.

23. For ESP, see for instance the controversy around the work of Daryl Bem, discussed in Daniel Engber, "Daryl Bem Proved ESP Is Real: Which Means Science Is Broken," *Slate*, June 7, 2017; for healing

prayer, see Candy Gunther Brown, *Testing Prayer* (Cambridge: Harvard University Press, 2012).

24. Matt. 4:7.

25. Freeman Dyson, "One in a Million," *New York Review of Books*, March 25, 2004, www.nybooks.com/articles/2004/03/25/one-in-a-million/.

26. The literature on near-death experiences is now voluminous, but the best recent introduction is Bruce Greyson, *After: A Doctor Explores What Near-Death Experiences Reveal about Life and Beyond* (New York: St. Martin's, 2021).

27. See, e.g., *The Illustrated Field Guide to DMT Entities: Machine Elves, Tricksters, Teachers, and Other Interdimensional Beings* (Rochester, VT: Park Street Press, February 2025) and Rick Strassman, *DMT: The Spirit Molecule* (Rochester, VT: Park Street Press, 2001). (More than in other areas of supernatural investigation, the tendency of researchers into hallucinogens to be enthusiastic participants in the experiments creates some consistent problems for analytic rigor.)

28. Sam Parnia et al., "Awareness during Resuscitation-II: A Multi-Center Study of Consciousness and Awareness in Cardiac Arrest," *Rescuscitation* 191 (October 2023).

29. Constanza Peinkhofer et al., "The Evolutionary Origin of Near-Death Experiences: A Systematic Investigation," *Brain Communications* 3, no. 3 (June 2021).

30. Shermer, *Heavens on Earth*, 118–19.

31. Shermer, *Heavens on Earth*, 118–19.

32. G. K. Chesterton, "The Maniac," *Orthodoxy*, chap. 2, www.gutenberg.org/cache/epub/130/pg130-images.html.

## Chapter 4: The Case for Commitment

1. Erik Hoel, *The World behind the World: Consciousness, Free Will, and the Limits of Science* (New York: Simon and Schuster, 2023), 158–59.

2. Rev. 3:16.

3. Philip Larkin, "Church Going," *The Less Deceived* (1954; London: Faber and Faber, 2011), 16–17.

4. Jules Evans, "Encounters with Negative Entities," *Ecstatic Integration*, September 28, 2023, www.ecstaticintegration.org/p/encounters-with-negative-entities. For a related discussion of demons surfacing in contemporary psychedelic therapy, see Robert Falconer, *The Others within Us, Internal Family Systems, Porous Mind, and Spirit Possession* (Great Mystery Press, 2023). For a materialist critique of Falconer, see Scott Alexander, "Book Review: The Others within Us," *Astral Star Codex*, May 21, 2024, www.astralcodexten.com/p/book-review-the-others-within-us.

## Chapter 5: Big Faiths and Big Divisions

1. Richard Dawkins, "Snake Oil and Holy Water," *Forbes*, October 4, 1999, www.forbes.com/asap/1999/1004/235.html.

2. David Hume, *An Inquiry Concerning Human Understanding*, section X: "Of Miracles," www3.nd.edu/~afreddos/courses/43811/hume-on-miracles.htm.

3. All such generalizations have fallen out of fashion, but for a compelling argument regarding patterns in primeval religion, see Marshall Sahlins, *The New Science of the Enchanted Cosmos* (Princeton: Princeton University Press, 2022). And for a discussion of how Sahlins' ghost kept appearing to his colleagues after his demise, see Anna Della Subin, "Metaperson: The Enchanted Worlds of Marshall Sahlins," *The Nation*, March 6, 2024.

4. W. H. Auden, "Advent," *For the Time Being: A Christmas Oratorio* (Princeton: Princeton University Press, 2013), 8.

5. T. M. Luhrmann, *How God Becomes Real: Kindling the Presence of Invisible Others* (Princeton: Princeton University Press, 2020).

6. Stephen Smith, *Pagans and Christians in the City: Culture Wars from the Tiber to the Potomac* (Grand Rapids: Eerdmans, 2018).

## Chapter 6: Three Stumbling Blocks

1. Job 38:4.
2. Thomas Paine, *Age of Reason*, "Conclusion," http://academic.brooklyn
   .cuny.edu/history/dfg/amrl/paine.htm.
3. Andrew Holt, "The Myth of Religious Violence as the Cause of
   Most Wars," in John D. Hosler, *Seven Myths of Military History*
   (Indianapolis: Hackett, 2022), https://apholt.com/2023/01/03/the
   -myth-of-religion-as-the-cause-of-most-wars/.
4. Damien Keown, *Buddhist Ethics: A Very Short Introduction* (Oxford:
   Oxford University Press, 2005), 50.

## Chapter 7: The End of Exploring

1. Ayaan Hirsi Ali, "Why I Am Now a Christian," *UnHerd*,
   November 11, 2023, https://unherd.com/2023/11/why-i-am-now-a
   -christian/.
2. Tyler Cowen, "Why I Don't Believe in God," *Marginal Revolution*,
   May 25, 2017, https://marginalrevolution.com/marginalrevolution
   /2017/05/dont-believe-god.html.
3. Matt. 25:29.
4. Paul Kingsnorth, "The Cross and the Machine," *First Things*, June
   2021, www.firstthings.com/article/2021/06/the-cross-and-the-machine.
5. T. S. Eliot, "Little Gidding," *Four Quartets*.
6. Eliot, "Little Gidding."

## Chapter 8: A Case Study: Why I Am a Christian

1. See e.g. Seraphim Rose, *The Soul after Death* (Platina, CA: St.
   Herman of Alaska Brotherhood, 2020).
2. Richard Bauckham, *Jesus and the Eyewitnesses: The Gospels as
   Eyewitness Testimony* (Grand Rapids: Eerdmans, 2017); N. T.
   Wright, *The Resurrection of the Son of God* (Minneapolis: Fortress
   Press, 2003); Peter J. Williams, *Can We Trust the Gospels?* (Wheaton,
   IL: Crossway, 2018).

3. Lydia McGrew, *Hidden in Plain View: Undesigned Coincidences in the Gospels and Acts* (Tampa, FL: DeWard, 2017).

4. Some of the scholarship may be slightly dated but I am partial to the arguments about the interrelationship of John and the synoptics in John A. T. Robinson, *The Priority of John* (Eugene, OR: Wipf and Stock Publishers, 2011).

5. See for example Michael Pakaluk, *The Memoirs of St. Peter: A New Translation of the Gospel according to Mark* (Washington, DC: Regnery, 2019).

6. C. S. Lewis, "Fern-Seed and Elephants," in *Fern-Seed and Elephants and Other Essays on Christianity* (Fontana: 1975), https://normangeisler.com/fernseeds-elephants/.

7. See the discussion of this phenomenon in Dale C. Allison Jr., *The Resurrection of Jesus: Apologetics, Polemic, History* (New York: Bloomsbury, 2021), ch. 12, "Rainbow Body."

8. Tom Holland, *Dominion: How the Christian Revolution Remade the World* (New York: Basic Books, 2019), 540–41.

9. Matt. 13:12.

10. Mark 13:35–36.